T4-ANG-712

BALANCED CHURCH GROWTH

BALANCED CHURCH GROWTH

Ebbie C. Smith

BROADMAN PRESS
Nashville, Tennessee

4262-46
ISBN: 0-8054-6246-5
Dewey Decimal Classification: 254.5
Subject Headings: CHURCH GROWTH
Library of Congress Catalog Card Number: 84-6456
Printed in the United States of America

Smith, Ebbie C.
Balanced church growth.

1. Church growth. I. Title.
BV652.25.S54 1984 254'.5 84-6456
ISBN 0-8054-6246-5

Dedicated to
Cal Guy
who has introduced so many
to the study of
missionary strategy

Contents

Foreword

This tremendous and most readable book should form a much-used part of every minister's library. Dr. Smith brilliantly highlights the biblical necessity of church growth. If Christians are true to the Bible, they must, like their Savior, seek and save the lost. They must bring back wandering sons and daughters to their Father's home. Every congregation and every denomination should be acutely aware of the vast numbers of the unchurched, the unsaved, the secularists, the materialists, and the worshipers of self, sex, money, and power. All these are lost, and a chief and irreplaceable part of the work of every Christian and every congregation must be to find the lost. They are God's children, and he wants them found.

Authentic church growth must also be balanced church growth. The title of this book is well chosen. Balanced church growth will emphasize in correct proportions the biblical mandates for church growth, the infilling of the Holy Spirit, the sociological structures of society, the psychological needs of men and women, and the organizational forms taken by beginning churches. The infilling of the Holy Spirit so often spoken of in the New Testament is an essential component of authentic church growth. When believers are filled with the Holy Spirit, then, even in the face of most adverse circumstances, they surge out to proclaim the gospel and multiply cells of believers.

One of the most wonderful verses in the New Testament is Acts 8:4. It tells of the Christians in Jerusalem who had been filled with the Holy Spirit on the Day of Pentecost, being so fiercely persecuted by Saul of Tarsus that they left the city and fled out across the Judean hills. As they fled, they went everywhere preaching the gospel. If those beaten, bloody, and ruined men and women could do that, so must the well fed, comfortable, car-borne Christians of the United States.

Balanced church growth, as Dr. Smith so well says, understands the social structures of that segment of mankind in which God has called them to work. Balanced church growth is filled with the Holy Spirit, uses effective methods, prays for God's blessing, endures in the face of difficulties, and never turns aside from efforts to seek and save the lost.

It is also true that authentic church growth recognizes that the methods used and the goals sought must be those which God blesses to the growth of his Church in particular pieces of the mosaic of mankind. What God will bless in one piece of the mosaic—let us say the hundreds of thousands of Hispanic illegals in California and Texas—will be quite different from the methods which he blesses to the increase of his Church among the professors in state universities. God blesses one approach in the animistic tribes of east Kenya or southern Nigeria where Baptists are multiplying churches and quite other approaches in the highly secularized "totally Christian" populations of Europe.

Balanced church growth constantly asks what approaches has God blessed and seeks to multiply them. This book is an excellent, clear, and convincing description of the many kinds of church growth which are authentically Christian and which God does bless. It will be read with great profit by thousands of lay leaders, ministers, and church executives.

DONALD MCGAVRAN

Introduction

Church growth is a term more often used than understood. In this day of staggering need and increasing possibilities, it is imperative that the concepts of church growth be thoroughly understood and its insights creatively applied. For these reasons, I will try to help you learn about the ways churches and denominations can and should grow. My concern has not been mere knowledge of facts about growing churches nor lists of books written on the subject. Rather, I have sought to learn what can be put into practice. My goal is that you will be able to help your church and other churches grow.

Throughout this book I distinguish between the Church Growth Movement and church growth strategy in general. I use the terms, *Church Growth Movement,* or *Church Growth Theory,* to refer to the body of teaching associated with the approach of Donald A. McGavran, Allan R. Tippett, C. Peter Wagner, Win Arn and others of the so-called, "Fuller School." This "theory" came into prominence around 1955 with the publication of McGavran's, *The Bridges of God.*

I use the terms, *Church Growth Specialist,* or *Church Growth Writer,* to refer to persons who follow the ideas of the Church Growth Movement. Incidentally, I consider myself one of these persons.

I use the term, *church growth,* or *church growth strategy* to refer to the methods, strategies, and means of helping churches grow. These strategies will not necessarily be drawn from, reflect, or depend on the teachings of the Church Growth Movement.

This book is intended neither as a restatement of nor a defense for the Church Growth Movement. I am discussing ways of achieving the growth of churches and denominations both in the United States and in other lands. In learning about church growth, my hope is that each insight and idea will be applied to each of our churches. May we attempt to understand how these strategies can help our churches grow.

Before we begin, let me mention some guidelines that will help our learning. When I use the term *Church* (capital C) I mean either the universal Church (Kingdom), organized Christianity, or a denomination. For example, "The Church exists in every nation," or "The Reformed Church in New England grew rapidly." When I use the term, *church* (lower case c) the meaning is a local congregation or an adjective. For example, "A church should grow bigger, better, and broader," or "We are discussing church growth."

The terms *Mission, mission,* and *missions* will also be used in distinctive ways. I use the term *mission* to refer to the mandate to world evangelism given by the Lord to his Church (and his churches). For example, "The Church's mission is to preach the gospel to every person." The term *missions* speaks of ways and means of carrying out the mission. For example, "In the face of increasing receptivity, missions must find new ways to present the gospel." The term *Mission* will be employed to speak of an organization of missionaries working together in a particular region. For example, "The Baptist Mission in Brazil promoted an evangelistic campaign," or "The Mission should promote new work."

Second, in speaking of church growth insights I am speaking basically about methods. The methods, or strategies, to attain church growth are not principles that must be followed in every place and time. They must be adjusted to situations. What works in Nigeria (among the Ibo) may be inappropriate in Chicago. Strategies that lead to harvest in Texas may result in resistance in Peru or Hong Kong (or even in Utah). Much misunderstanding will be avoided if we remember that church growth basically speaks of methods and methods that can be altered, set aside, or used as the situation demands.

Third, persons seeking church growth must understand and gratefully acknowledge the necessity of the Holy Spirit for any spiritual harvest. Leaders desiring church growth need to find those methods that are most effectively used by the Holy Spirit in each situation to bring about the maximum increase of responsible believers who are gathered into responsible congregations. Finding these methods is the task of church growth studies.

So, let's learn about church growth.

Questions and Activities

1. Describe the goal and purpose of the study of church growth.
2. What is the difference between the Church Growth Movement and church growth in general?
3. Use the terms, *Church, church, mission, missions,* and *Mission* as they will be used in this book.
4. Respond to the charge that church growth overlooks the Holy Spirit and depends only on methods and strategies.

1
Catching the Vision for Growth

Vision is a requisite for church growth. Vision is the capacity to see both needs and possibilities. With vision one perceives opportunities for growth when another, lacking vision, succumbs to complacency or depression and gives up. In reality, vision is the ability to dream—or in some cases to dream again.

Effective church growth depends on vision for growth. Until church leaders catch this vision and grasp clearly both the needs and possibilities, growth is improbable if not impossible. Catching the vision for growth is, therefore, an imperative first step in achieving church growth.

Defining Church Growth

An accurate definition of church growth stimulates a vital vision for growth. The words *church* and *growth* have meanings independent of one another. When the two are used together, however, they assume a specialized meaning. The term *church growth* refers to the application of methods and strategies to further the numerical and qualitative growth of local congregations and denominations. Church growth studies seek to discover facts and truths which lead to priorities, goals, and strategies that increase the overall growth of churches (and Churches). An adequate definition of church growth includes at least eight factors.

An important first factor in a definition of church growth relates to the numerical increase of churches and of members in churches. The full meaning of church growth, to be sure, goes beyond the numerical increase of members and congregations. Only the most limited concept of church growth restricts the idea of growth to the increase of names on church rolls. Numerical increase in both Christians and congregations is, however, an important factor in church growth and must neither be neglected nor overlooked. Seeking numerical increase of both churches and church members is a spiritual undertaking and must always receive adequate attention.

Evangelism constitutes an important second factor in a definition of church growth. Church growth emphasizes winning all people and groups of people (ethnic, national, language, socio-economic, regional) on earth to faith in Christ. Evangelizing means bringing people to a personal, saving knowledge of Jesus Christ to the end they become his followers and members of his Church and one of his churches.

Other Church Growth Writers use the term *discipling* rather than *evangelizing* to speak of bringing the lost to Christ. Discipling may well be more accurate than evangelizing for leading persons to the initial experience of salvation in Jesus. In this book, however, I will use the term *evangelizing* to speak of winning persons to Christ and *discipling* to refer to the efforts of guiding believers toward maturity in the faith. Church Growth Writers usually employ the term *perfecting* for this maturing process. Keeping in mind this usage of evangelizing/discipling, and discipling/perfecting will help not only as you read this book but also other Church Growth materials as well.

Church growth teaches that the purpose of evangelism is "making disciples" not simply the registering of decisions. Becoming a disciple (follower) of Jesus involves committing the entire life to him and his way of living. Discipleship means changing from the self-centered, worldly existence to the life-style exemplified by Jesus. Evangelizing and discipling cannot be separated. They are parts of the same process. True evangelism, as taught by church growth, seeks to guide people to this experience of life-changing relationship with God in Christ. This unified concept of evangelism lies at the heart of church growth thinking and must be a part of a definition of church growth.

A definition of church growth must also include the factor of the spiritual incorporation of the evangelized into local congregations of worshiping, serving believers. Church growth remains incomplete until believers are vitally related to a local body of Christians. Spiritual incorporation means the believer becomes a part of the local body of Christ as the mind and body are part of a physical organism. Christians must be incorporated into both the membership and fellowship of a Christian congregation and church growth remains unfinished until this has happened.

Churches which follow church growth patterns pay close attention to the incorporation of believers into the body. Converts in the New Testament period were added to the church (Acts 2:41-42). This bonding was so complete that believers held all possessions in common and distributed to the needs of each person in the fellowship (Acts 2:45-46; 4:32-33). The necessity of this spiritual incorporation provided an important reason for guarding the unity of the churches (1 Cor. 12—14; Phil. 2:1-11). Any approach to church growth that fails to provide for the spiritual incorporation of believers into the local fellowships falls drastically short of authentic church growth.

A fourth factor in a definition of church growth relates to discipling or perfecting of believers in the congregations. Believers in the New Testament churches continued in the apostles' doctrine and fellowship (Acts 2:42). Individual Christian growth remains an important factor in church growth. In fact, any church growth methodology that does not provide for discipling believers must be classified defective church growth.

To be more specific, some consider a church to be doing well if it baptizes hundreds. If, however, this church shows little or no increase in attendance, dedication, or service, the growth is open to question. If the members show little or no progress in Christian living there is likewise a question as to the validity of the growth. A mother remarked that conceiving and birthing a child is the easiest part of parenting. The real challenge comes in nurturing and guiding the child to Christian maturity. Church growth sees the same phenomenon regarding both disciples and congregations. The most demanding and creative efforts are required for strengthening persons won and congregations planted.

In defining church growth it is important to note that the strategies and methods suggested have been discovered rather than created. Ideas embodied in church growth thinking have been in existence and have been in use since New Testament times. Church Growth Specialists have not created ideas about or strategies for church growth. They have found these insights by studying churches that are growing, churches that are stagnant, and churches that are declining. From these studies, have come insights for strategies that make up Church Growth Theory.

The fact that church growth ideas have been discovered in the field and do not represent some theory based on conjecture adds significance to the teachings. Church growth concepts are the fruit of careful observation and study. Any definition of church growth must include this fifth factor, that is, the discovered nature of church growth ideas.

Reproducibility constitutes a sixth factor in the definition of church growth. Genuine church growth requires that both Christians and churches continuously produce more Christians and more congregations. This expansion is achieved by the continuing witness of believers and the constant multiplication of congregations. Genuine church growth reproduces; only reproducing and reproducible church growth is acceptable.

Church growth teaches that methodology that either hinders or fails to provide for the constant increase of Christians and churches is invalid strategy. Any strategy that fails to build in reproducibility hinders continuing expansion. Subsidy, an often-used missionary method, usually renders reproducibility impossible. Failure to teach personal soul-winning leads to spiritual infertility. Proper church growth strategy demands and provides for the constant multiplication of churches and Christians.

A seventh factor in a definition of church growth relates to the use of appropriate methods. Church growth constantly seeks methods that enhance the desired end of church advance. Models for these strategies are drawn, not only from biblical teachings, but from sociological, anthropological, business, and many other disciplines as well. This fact does not, however, mean that any method that produces growth is acceptable nor that the end (growth) justifies any means that might be used. Every method must be an acceptable method.

To be acceptable, a method must conform to biblical teachings and produce a biblically valid result. Conformity to biblical teachings does not demand a strategy be directly mentioned in Scripture. One might be hard pressed to find Sunday School departments, women's organizations, mission boards, or family life centers directly mentioned in the Bible. All of these methods have been and are being used appropriately because they are compatible with biblical teachings.

Some methods, however, do not conform to biblical teachings. For example, some leaders manipulate people into registering decisions and even accepting baptism. Such methods may produce numerical growth in the form of more names on the church roll but they violate the biblical principles of the integrity and value of persons created in the image of God and the nature of salvation. Any such methodology must be rejected as both inappropriate and inauthentic strategy.

Other strategies lead to nonbiblical results and, hence, must be rejected as inappropriate. It is possible to place such stress on spiritual growth and development that meaningful contact with the world is lost. The resulting divorce of "self" from "world" leads to unevangelistic churches and nonreproducing Christians. A group can place such emphasis on reaching our kind of people that they lose missionary vision. Again, the unbiblical result is apparent. Any method that eventuates in an unbiblical result must be rejected. Church growth approves only appropriate methods which conform to biblical standards and produce biblically valid results.

Finally, an adequate definition of church growth involves the factor of continuously monitoring and evaluating the results of church growth efforts. Monitoring and evaluating processes seek to understand effectiveness in order to implement further development. Everything the church, or Church, does should be open to scrutiny in this effort to improve. Nothing should be beyond the reach of change if change gives promise of increasing the harvest. Constant monitoring and evaluating for the purpose of recognizing need and achieving change is a vital part of church growth thinking.

What then do we mean by church growth? Church growth is that body of discovered, biblically appropriate and biblically based strategies that relate to the numerical increase and spiritual development of churches and Christians through fulfilling the mandates of evangelizing, discipling, incorporating, and evaluating to ensure continued progress and ministry.

Expecting Church Growth

Many Churches (and churches) are locked in a status of non-growth or even decline. Expecting little growth they achieve it; aiming at meager advance, they hit it; accepting slow increase as the norm, they are content with it. These attitudes toward growth are not biblical and certainly not pleasing to God. Church growth projects optimism, believing that we can and should expect growth.

Today is the best of times for church growth. There are more winnable people and more resources for winning them than at any other period of history. Obedience to the will of God and confidence in the power of the Holy Spirit leads to the expectations for church growth. The Church today needs to hear again William Carey's cry, "Attempt great things for God, expect great things from God."

This expectation of growth stems partly from the conviction that God wants his churches to grow. In the Garden, after mankind's initial transgression, God came seeking and finding the errant Adam and Eve (see Gen. 3:8-24). In the parables, Jesus stressed the importance of finding and bringing the lost to the Lord. The woman seeks until the lost coin is found. The shepherd returns, rejoicing, because the lost sheep is found. The father waits at the gate, longing for the son's return and rejoices in that return (see Luke

15:3-32). Obviously, finding the lost and returning them to the Lord's presence is the will of the Father. It is also the goal of church growth.

By expecting increase, church growth espouses harvest rather than search theology. Search theology conceives seed-sowing, good deeds, social service, or mere presence among the lost to be the essence of missions. It can be characterized as pre-evangelism. Bringing people to faith in Christ and starting churches is a secondary concern to those who follow search theology.

Harvest theology, on the other hand, considers the salvation of individuals and the planting of congregations the essence of missions. Social ministry, good deeds, and helping are important Christian acts but should never replace the priority of finding the lost. According to harvest theology, the primary task is to participate in God's vast finding.

Biblical teachings solidly support the conviction that God wants church growth. Few passages are plainer than the Great Commission (see Matt. 28:16-20). Verses 19-20 should be translated:

> As you go, make disciples of all the peoples, baptizing them in the name of the Father, and of the Son, and of the Holy Spirit: teaching them to observe all things which I have commanded you; and remember, I am with you until the end of the age.

The direct imperative in the command is in the verb, "make disciples." Three participles, "going," "baptizing," and "teaching," describe how or the means by which this discipling (including evangelizing and maturing in the faith) is to be achieved. Clearly, the Great Commission involves winning, discipling, and training followers of Christ.

The Book of Acts reveals a record of numerical increase as it describes the rapid growth of the New Testament churches. The Christian group began as a company of 120 persons (Acts 1:15). On the Day of Pentecost, 3,000 souls were added (Acts 2:41-42). In Acts 4:4 Luke records that after imprisonment, persecution, and threat, the disciples prayed for boldness to preach the gospel and the company increased to 5,000 men. A chapter later in Acts, the emphasis turned to multitudes of men and women who were incorporated into the fellowship (5:14). In Acts 6:1-7 the report is that the number of disciples multiplied.

By chapter 9, Acts begins to report the increase in the number of churches as well as members. The number of congregations in Judea, Samaria, and Galilee is said to have multiplied (Acts 9:31). In Acts 16:5 the change from church to churches underscores the place of organized Christian fellowships (churches) in the development of God's missionary plan. Finally, Paul used the term *myriads* (10,000) to describe the growth of the churches (Acts 21:20). Clearly, tens of thousands of persons turned to Christ and became members of his churches.

The Bible not only supports church growth, it demands it. God's will is that his churches grow. God's will forms the dynamic motivation in the believer's life. We expect church growth because God promises it; we strive for church growth because God wants it.

We expect growth because growth is normal for an organism. Healthy bodies grow; healthy churches grow. When spiritual climate is vital, churches find ways of growing. Many Christians see growing churches as the unusual, the different. Actually, it is the growing church which is reacting normally to the vast possibilities of growth in the world. Unlimited power and potential for growth are available from God.

Some churches find growth limited by factors beyond their control. Some churches, located in areas of declining population, may find their numerical growth more limited than churches in regions of expanding population. Churches in transitional communities may find growth among their kind of people restricted. Churches in resistant areas, where the people are hard as flint against the gospel, may experience limited growth. We must not, however, accept these situations as the norm and certainly not as the ideal.

In other cases, growth is possible but churches and Christians are content with meager increase. Excuses for nongrowth are more often heard in these churches than are plans for harvest. Hindrances to growth do not relieve churches of the responsibility to grow. It is imperative that churches not be content with limited numerical growth when possibilities for more abundant harvest exist. Often the limitation on growth lies more within the church than with the people to be reached. Unfounded excuses should not disguise the normalcy of growth nor eclipse the expectation for growth.

Many excuses for failing to grow are offered, but none are legitimate. The idea that we do a better quality job than some other group should never be used to justify our failure to grow. In regard to excuses, it is instructive to read again the parable of the talents. Note, those who had performed in accordance with the will of the Lord reported in only thirteen words, "Master, you left five bags with me; look, I have made five more" (Matt. 25:20, NEB). On the other hand, the one who had failed to perform required forty-six words to excuse his neglect (Matt. 25:24-25). Such is the nature of most excuses for not growing.

Church growth should be characterized by optimism. Growth rather than stagnation is the normal pattern for the Lord's churches. God expects growth. The Lord Jesus promises growth. The Holy Spirit provides power for growth. Vision for growth develops as we allow God to create within us an expectation of authentic church growth.

Refining the Concept of Growth

Vision for growth develops properly only in company with a correct concept of growth. The concept of growth must, therefore, be refined before vision can evolve. An inaccurate concept of growth stifles vision by allowing churches and leaders to consider their group to be growing when the growth is actually invalid. Faulty concepts of growth blind church people to vaster harvest that may be going ungathered. Invalid concepts of growth may lead to diagnosis of health when the church is actually sick. Refining the concept of growth corrects inaccurate assessments and thereby produces vision.

"Our church is really growing," reported a pastor. "In the past six months we have received 300 new members." This would seem a record of rapid growth. A refining look, however, indicates that of the 300 additions, 270 were transfers from other churches (or what is called transfer growth). Growth by transfer means every new member in one church represents one less member in some other church. Moreover, of the 30 baptisms, 24 were children of members (or what is called biological growth). In this "growing church" only one person per month had been won from the world. These six persons, added by what is called conversion growth, are not more important than the others. Transfer and biological growth are important for God's Kingdom. But conversion growth must be given a more prominent place in churches for it is by conversion growth that the Kingdom increases most rapidly.

Refining the concept of growth demands that records reflect the additions achieved by transfer, biological, and conversion patterns. Churches relying on transfer and biological growth with little conversion growth are experiencing less than authentic church growth. Most churches are long on transfer and biological and short on conversion growth. Viewing records of additions from the vantage of the three kinds of growth helps refine the concept of growth.

Growth figures should also be refined to indicate the relationship between additions and commitment to the Lord's service and his church. One church reported over 800 baptisms in a year. The same year this church also recorded a decrease in both Bible study enrollment and attendance. Another church in a three-year period baptized more people than it had enrolled in Bible study at the end of the three-year period. The growth record of this church showed more additions during this three-year period than attendance at its worship services on any Sunday. In both cases, the record of growth should have been questioned and refined.

Only lasting church growth is authentic church growth. Bringing unsaved people to the church and adding their names to the church roll when there is no change in life or commitment to the Lord's service is neither acceptable church growth nor the goal of church growth strategy.

Denominations, like local churches, should refine their concept of growth. A denomination that boasts thousands of members but finds that over 30 percent of its members live in communities other than that served by their church must look carefully at the validity of the growth. A Church that finds the resident-member-to-baptism ratio to be 30 to 1 must accept the fact that commitment is lagging. No group should too easily accept the conclusion of adequate growth until the concept of growth has been refined.

Growth figures must also be refined to show the church's (or Church's) growth rate as compared to population growth. A denomination should be brought to its knees by the realization that its growth lags behind population increase. In 1970 Southern Baptists in the Houston, Texas, area had one church for every 6,865 persons. In 1979 the figure had become one church for every 10,000 persons and if trends continue by 1990 will be one church for every 18,000 persons. Southern Baptists had 11.7 percent of the people in the Houston area in their churches in 1970 but that figure had fallen to 8.6 percent by 1979. If the trend continues, Southern Baptists will have only 5.9 percent of the population in their churches by 1990.[1] Refining information in this way should lead to changes in strategy and commitment.

The comparison of church to community growth should include consideration of the racial, social, economic, or life-style changes that may be taking place in the community. Communities change. The characteristics of the people living in the community also change. Every church and denomination should carefully monitor the areas served to ascertain if the church is maintaining contact with every segment of the population in the community. There may be a need to expand the kinds of ministry to meet new demands. Refining of information in this way greatly adds to a vision for growth.

Refining growth figures can reveal strengths as well as weaknesses in a church's ministry. A church that reports 250 new members each year over a period of years and yet remains on a plateau in membership figures might appear to show inauthentic growth. If, however, study reveals this church had started several missions, giving up members each time as seed families to the new work, the growth pictured is commendable.

Refining the concept of growth answers the question, "Are we really growing?" Favorable records do not always indicate authentic growth. Realization of evangelistic needs and the inadequacy of church response should stimulate efforts toward authentic church growth. Refining the concept of growth, therefore, remains a rewarding and productive undertaking in preparing the ground for church growth. Vision is caught when the concept of growth is refined.

Accept the Challenge for Church Growth

Few experiences excite vision for church growth more profoundly than seeing the world's need for and accepting the challenge of that need. Almost 75 percent of the world's people do not worship Jesus Christ. More than one person a second dies without him. The number of people, and consequently, the number of lost people in the world, continues to expand with unbelievable swiftness. Edward R. Dayton graphically presents the rapidity of this population increase pointing out that in the 1500 years between the time of Jesus and Martin Luther, world population doubled from 250 to 500 million. By the time William Carey sailed for India in 1793, the population had doubled again—this time in only 250 years. By 1910, the time of the Edinburgh Missionary Conference, world population had doubled once more and stood at just over two billion. Since 1910 population has already more than doubled and if it continues to expand will be somewhere between six and seven billion by 2000.[2]

The need for salvation on the part of three of every four persons in the world challenges believers everywhere to renewed evangelism. This challenge is compounded by the fact that of the slightly more than one billion Christians, only about 200 million are estimated to be dedicated, committed, practicing church members. Among the 979 million many are nominal, marginal Christians. Others are actually unsaved with their names on some church roll. These people must be won by E-O evangelism, a Church

Growth expression for evangelism aimed at renewing existing Christians or winning church members who have never experienced personal salvation.[3]

There are around 336 million (13%) of the 2.4 billion lost people in the world who live in areas where there are churches made up of Christians of basically the same cultural or linguistic groupings as the lost. These 336 million lost persons can be evangelized by E-1 evangelism, that is, by the witness of near neighbors of similar language and culture.[4]

This leaves over two billion lost people who can only be reached by cross-cultural evangelism. Church Growth Writers call evangelism across extreme cultural boundaries E-2 evangelism. Evangelism which attempts to cross even more extreme cultural boundaries is called E-3 evangelism.[5] The challenge projected by world need is yet more acutely seen in Dayton's statement that even if all the churches in the world were to reach out to their unsaved neighbors with all fervency, only one third of the people of the world would hear the gospel from Christians who speak their language and understand their culture.[6] The challenge of this worldwide need must excite the vision for church growth.

The challenge can likewise be seen in the United States where the need for church growth continues to mount. In 1980 there were 231,708 churches in the United States with 112,538,310 adherents. This figure constituted 49.7 percent of the people in the nation. Note, however, that adherents represented the total community of the churches—including small children and other family members. When figures for communicant, confirmed members are cited we find 48,834,482 church members.[7] Obviously, a vast harvest awaits in the United States.

Thus, over one half of the people in the United States are unchurched. More frightening still, is the dismal record of churches and denominations in the United States in recent years. Decline in both membership and attendance has been obvious in the records of many, if not most, denominations in the United States since the 1960s.[8] Carl S. Dudley contends that many people who are religious and testify to a relationship with the Lord are alienated from the churches.[9] Lost and strayed persons constitute a mission field in every community in the United States.

Vision for growth should be stimulated by a realization of the worldwide need for Christ and the ministry of churches. Accepting the need and challenge of church growth should compel Christians to plant churches and win converts.

Conclusion

The massive increase of Christians and churches needed in the world today awaits an immense expansion of a vision for growth in the hearts and minds of Christians and churches. This vision for church growth springs from a correct understanding of the nature of growth, a realization that God wants growth and has provided for it by the Spirit, an accurate picture of the status of growth in any church or denomination, and an acceptance of the worldwide need for church growth. Catching the vision for growth is the vital first step in achieving authentic, God-pleasing church growth.

Questions and Activities

1. Write a paragraph explaining what the term church growth means. Be certain to use all eight factors.
2. What is your dream for your church? Share it with someone.
3. Study the additions to your church during the last two years. How many were the result of transfer growth? Of biological growth? Of conversion growth?
4. What is the ratio between resident members and baptisms in your church?
5. List several strategies you feel would not be appropriate for any church to use. List several new strategies you wish your church would use.

Further Reading

Gerber, Virgil. *God's Way to Keep a Church Going and Growing* (Revell)
McGavran, Donald A., and Arn, Win. *Ten Steps to Church Growth* (Harper and Row)
———. *How to Grow a Church* (Regal)
Wagner, C. Peter. *Your Church Can Grow* (Regal)
Dale, Robert H. *To Dream Again* (Broadman)
McGavran, Donald A. *Understanding Church Growth* (Eerdmans)
Hunter, George III. *The Contagious Congregation* (Abingdon)
Miller, Calvin. *A View from the Fields* (Broadman)

Notes

1. Chester B. Davidson, "Associational Resource Data, Key Area 3," (Houston, Tex.: Baptist Association Correlating Committee, 1980).

2. Edward R. Dayton, "To Reach the Unreached," in *Unreached Peoples '79* ed. by C. Peter Wagner and Edward R. Dayton (Elgin, Ill.: David C. Cook Publishing Co., 1978), pp. 17-18.

3. Donald A. McGavran, *Understanding Church Growth* (Grand Rapids: Wm. B. Eerdmans Publishing Co., 1980), pp. 63-66.

4. Ibid.

5. Ibid., p. 64.

6. Dayton, p. 21.

7. Bernard Quinn, Herman Anderson, Martin Bradley, Paul Goetting, and Peggy Shriver. *Churches and Church Membership in the United States 1980* (Atlanta, Ga.: Glenmary Research Center, 1982), p. xiii, 1-2.

8. David A. Roozen and Jackson W. Carroll, "Recent Trends in Church Membership and Participation: An Introduction," in *Understanding Church Growth and Decline, 1950-1978,* ed. Dean R. Hoge and David A. Roozen (New York: The Pilgrim Press, 1979), pp. 21-41.

9. Carl S. Dudley, *Where Have All the People Gone?* (New York: The Pilgrim Press, 1979), pp. 19, 41-42.

2
Centering on the Basics of Church Growth

Back to the basics has become the rallying cry for almost every sphere of activity. Even professional athletes devote early practices to basics. Learning about church growth is likewise best achieved by grasping the meaning and significance of basic concepts and ideas.

The basic concepts in my approach to church growth are: the "bridges of God," a balanced approach, effective evangelism, the unlimited multiplication of churches, and reliance on the Holy Spirit. Church growth thinking begins with and must center on these basic concepts.

The "Bridges of God"

One basic concept in church growth thinking, the "Bridges of God," provided the title and central idea in Donald A. McGavran's bombshell book in 1955. So central is this idea that McGavran calls finding the "bridges" the key strategy in church growth.[1] The dean of the Church Growth School describes the idea of the "bridges of God" saying,

> the faith spreads most naturally and contagiously along the lines of the social network of living Christians, especially new Christians. Receptive undiscipled men and women usually receive the Possibility when the invitation is extended to them from credible Christian friends, relatives, neighbors, and fellow workers from within their social web.[2]

The reality of the faith expanding along relationship lines can be seen in the New Testament record (see John 1:40-42; 4:39-42; Mark 5:19; Acts 16:13-15). The phenomenon has been experienced often in missionary activity outside the United States. McGavran first grasped the idea of the "bridges" in India. He later discovered the same pattern in Africa, Latin America, and Asia. Win Arn and Lyle R. Schaller, authorities on American church growth, recognize the "bridges" pattern in the growth of churches in this land.[3]

Missionary history indicates that the most rapid increase of believers and churches occurs when the faith spreads naturally between people who are already associated in a particular social unit and between social units in a population. Bridges of God are, then, avenues of communication and relationship over which the gospel flows from one person to another and from one group to another.

The idea of evangelism and church growth along relationship lines can be diagramed.

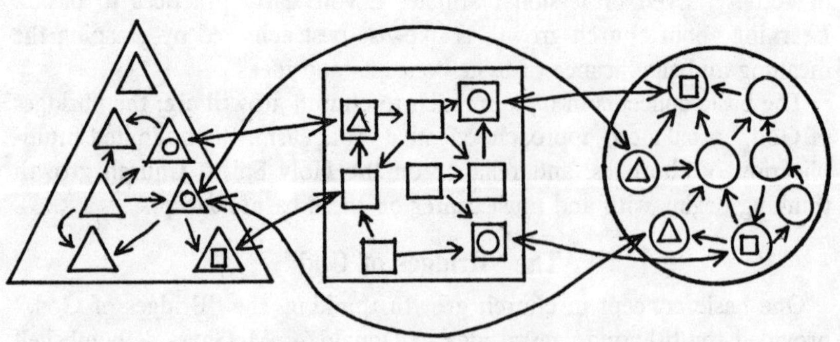

In the diagram, the square, the triangle, and the circle represent social networks of persons. Persons within each of the networks are represented by squares, triangles, and circles. Relationships between these persons are depicted by the arrows. These relationships provide bridges over which the message easily flows. Following these bridges, the gospel effectively moves through a social grouping. Missionaries in Indonesia were surprised to find the churches composed largely of persons connected either by family, friendship, or some other associations. They should not have been surprised. It was only the outworking of the bridges of God.

If only the bridges within one social grouping are followed, the movement will stall as it reaches the outer limits of that social network. Too often, new congregations reach a certain level, and growth either slows drastically or in some cases stops altogether. Missionaries sometimes ask, "Why do our churches grow rapidly to thirty or fifty members and then plateau?" The reason may be stalling at the edge of a social network.

The diagram also shows some members in the networks who have more than one alignment. The square-triangle and triangle-circle diagrams indicate individuals within the square network. Their primary relationships are with other square-related (or circle or triangle) individuals, but these persons also have personal relationships with persons in the triangle, square, or circle groups. These relationships (see arrows) are bridges to persons in the triangle and circle networks who are depicted triangle-square and circle-square. For a movement to continue growing, it is imperative that these bridges between groups be sought, found, and followed. Continued expansion is possible only as the cross-network bridges are fully exploited.

The pattern described is clearly seen in the growth of the church in East Java in the 1800s. C. L. Coolen, a Dutch planter, evangelized the Javanese working on his plantation. Relationships between some of Coolen's workers and a group of religious seekers who met in the home of Pak Dasimah, led to one of this group hearing and responding to the gospel. From this convert the faith flowed to other members of the group in Pak Dasimah's house. Later, other relationships between members of Pak Dasimah's congregation and Christians in the city of Surabaya, led to a connection between the two groups. Thus the Church in East Java was born by following both the intra and inter-group bridges of God.[4]

The bridges of God constitute a basic philosophy in church growth strategy. The growth of a Sunday School class, a new church, an existing church, or a denomination can be enhanced by using the bridges existing in the members' social networks.

Two matters must, however, be kept clearly in mind. First, the growth of any group can be seriously curtailed unless the intergroup bridges are recognized and followed. Second, the bridges of God are not the only pattern for evangelism. Many souls are won to Christ when approached by Christians whom they have not known before. The strategy of relationship evangelism does not rule out witnessing to persons outside the range of acquaintances. It does suggest that finding, following and using the bridges is a valid strategy that can significantly enhance church growth.

A first basic in church growth strategy is the pattern of the bridges of God.

Balanced Church Growth

The XYZ Corporation experienced unusual growth and expansion. Outlets were multiplied while products and services were added. The financial and organizational base did not, however, maintain balance with the increase in services and outlets. Needless to say, the corporation soon ran into serious problems. The lack of balance in the growth pattern led to the eventual failure of the enterprise.

Balance is as important for church growth as it is for any other endeavor. Church growth emphasizes numerical increase of members in churches and the multiplication of congregations. The Church's mission centers on finding and winning people to Christ and gathering them into churches. Church growth does not, however, as some believe, restrict its concern to numerical increase.

Any church or denomination that continues to grow bigger without at the same time growing better by expanding its base to care for the numerical increase will face serious consequences. Balance is basic for authentic church growth. Churches must maintain balance between growing bigger, better, and broader. Growing bigger involves adding members and congregations. Growing better includes increasing the church's ability to carry out its mission and care for the spiritual maturing of its members. Growing broader covers the ministry and missionary dimensions of the church's task.[5] All three types of growth are imperative. None can be neglected; none should overshadow the others.

Growing Bigger

Church growth is dedicated to the numerical increase of believers and the churches into which they are gathered. Numerical increase lies at the heart of God's will for his churches. Every number represents a person brought to the Lord. It matters that the lost are found. Growing bigger is important.

While an indispensable element in church growth, numerical increase is not the sole criterion of growth. As seen earlier, only lasting growth is proper church growth. Further, balance must be maintained between transfer, biological, and conversion patterns. Balance is required even in the search for numerical increase.

Churches possess a variety of avenues by which to attain numerical growth. A church (or Church) can grow bigger as a result of experiencing revival. Revival, in this sense, refers to a renewing of spiritual life, a recommitment to God's purposes, a purging of sin through the Spirit. Groups of missionaries have seen fruitfulness multiply in the wake of spiritual renewal. Denominations have experienced marvelous increase after the winds of revival have blown. Local churches have seen growth return when revival led to the overthrow of sin. Effective, lasting numerical increase is built on the base of revival.

Growth of the Church on the Island of Nias, Indonesia, was slow from 1874 until 1921. After fifty years the church reached 20,000 members. Between 1915 and 1921, the membership of the Church tripled reaching over 62,000. A major reason for this great ingathering was the *fangesa dodo* or great repentance. A revival swept the Christians on Nias leading to renewal in the Church.[6]

The churches on the Indonesian island, Timor, had become cold, worldly, unconcerned, and indifferent. Then about 1964 revival came. Unconcern changed to compassion. Worldliness changed to dedication; nominal churches changed to missionary bodies. While some stories of miraculous events related to this revival may have been overreported, the undeniable truth is that thousands were swept into the Kingdom and the churches.[7]

The accounts of churches on Nias and Timor reveal the place of revival in growing bigger. Revival remains a basic component for any group of Christians desiring to grow bigger.

A church can also reach numerical growth by emphasizing winnable people. Church growth does not advocate restricting evangelistic efforts to the responsive and certainly would not condone neglecting the resistant. Church growth thinking does, however, insist that priority be given to the responsive. Reap the harvest when God prepares it and the Spirit provides it. Continue to serve the resistant. Who knows but in the providence of God they may turn responsive. But the main efforts and the bulk of the resources should be used in the fields where the Spirit is granting growth.

In 1840 American Baptists began a mission at Nellore on the east coast of India. After twenty-five years laboring among the upper castes, they could point to less than one hundred converts. In 1865 John Clough and his wife turned to the Madigas (untouchables). By 1878 over 12,800 Madigas had come to Christ and into the Church.[8] Turning to the winnable and emphasizing evangelism among the responsive enables the church to grow bigger.

A church can reach toward numerical growth by turning to productive strategy. To remain chained to an unproductive method when a more productive is available is basically unfaithfulness to the Lord of the harvest. Numerical growth can be impeded by continued use of ineffective methods. Charles L. Chaney describes how changing to a strategy of aggressive church planting based on sound research into needs and possibilities led to exciting church growth among Southern Baptist churches in Illinois.[9]

A church can grow bigger by properly emphasizing numbers. Numbering, that is counting members, baptisms, congregations, and other facts about churches, is neither right or wrong in itself. Counting for self-glorification, or to bring recognition to person or denomination is obviously wrong. On the other hand, if numbering is done to understand the situation in order to do a more effective ministry, then numbering is not only proper, it is necessary. Careful numbering remains an imperative strategy in church growth thinking. As Alan R. Tippett said:

> The motive for the careful numbering required in mission statistics is not pride in our accomplishments but the recognition of the seriousness of the commission given to us lesser shepherds to "care for the flock of God" until the "Chief Shepherd comes" (1 Peter 5:2-4). Good numbering is part of good shepherding.[10]

The goal of numerical growth is vital. The final goal of growing bigger is not a superchurch. Some Church Growth Writings give the idea that the goal of church growth is a superchurch and only those attaining to superchurch status have reached success. Peter Wagner holds up several of the larger congregations as prime examples of church growth.[11] Without playing down the importance of these huge churches, I would like to say that I do not believe the superchurch is either the only way nor the ideal way to grow the Lord's Church.

Larger churches have some advantages. Smaller churches also have advantages, not the least of these being evangelistic effectiveness. Philip Barron Jones points out that Southern Baptist churches less than twelve years old and less than fifty members, reported 11.4 baptisms per 100 resident members. Churches with over 3,000 members and forty-one or more years of existence reported 3.5 baptisms per 100 resident members.[12]

Smallness alone does not lead to evangelistic effectiveness, spiritual fervor, or effective ministry. In Jones' study, churches of fifty members or less with forty-one years in existence reported only 3.3 baptisms per 100 resident members.[13] The point is not bigness or smallness. Every denominaton needs many large, many small, and many mid-sized churches. The point is that a superchurch is neither the one-and-only goal of church growth nor always the best expression of church growth.

I believe a better overall pattern of denominational growth results when there are many mid-sized churches rather than a few superchurches.

Churches should grow more and more rather than just larger and larger. The church that remains stationary in membership totals but starts several missions is growing larger. Every denomination must seek a balance between the larger, medium, and smaller-size churches. Most important, equal dignity, honor, and emphasis must be given the various sized churches and those who are called to labor in them.

Churches and denominations must seek to grow bigger by adding members and congregations. Even the efforts to grow bigger should be kept in balance. Growing bigger without growing better and broader is never the goal of church growth. Balance is a key concept in church growth thinking.

Growing Better

Growing bigger does not exhaust either the growth needs or potentials of churches. Churches must also grow better. Churches grow better by developing members' spiritual quality and ability to serve, by increasing the church's capacity to carry out the functions of worship, care, influence, ministry, and evangelism, and by expanding the church's ability to live as the Body of Christ. Every church must devise methods for growing better.

The Church Growth Movement has admittedly centered on numerical increase of Christians and churches. McGavran and his followers have attempted to awaken religious groups who had lost evangelistic and missionary fervor to the needs and possibilities of growth. Church Growth Writers have opposed philosophies of mission that set aside "Great Commission Missions," that is, missions that seek a response to the invitation to salvation and church membership.

This needed and proper emphasis on growing bigger has not, however, caused a total neglect of the emphasis on quality growth. Tippett has said, "The incorporation of large numbers of converts without provision for their spiritual nurture has never been allowed in church growth theory."[14] The time has come for Church Growth Thinkers to place more emphasis on the qualitative growth of churches and Christians.

In the effort to grow better, a church must provide for the spiritual nurture and practical training of every member. Bible and doctrinal study are indispensable in developing spiritual health. Christian fellowship strengthens believers. Training in Christian service and the provision of opportunities to serve must be a vital part of efforts toward growing better. Soul-winning, more than any other factor in Christian living, contributes to the spiritual development of the one witnessing. Any effort to grow better must include motivation to and training for the great opportunity of sharing faith in Christ. Only as each member is developing can the church feel that it is progressing toward the goal of qualitative church growth.

A church growing better does not automatically demand more elaborate facilities. The provision of needed services to the members is more important than erecting impressive buildings. A developing church expands its ability to serve as the Body of Christ. Some churches become so entangled in providing facilities that they neglect the care of the "body."

Mistakes can be made at both ends of the effort at growing better. A church that places total emphasis on growing bigger and gives little or no consideration to the spiritual nurture and training of members will lose the capacity to continue numerical increase. On the other hand, a church that centers on the maturing or discipling of members to the neglect of growing bigger will find itself in decline—both numerically and spiritually.

A common error of both churches and denominations that leads to undue stress on quality growth is expressed, "We must grow better before we can grow bigger." Another expression of the same attitude is, "We must strengthen the churches we have before we start any new congregations." Others say, "The churches we already have are so weak and need so much help, it does not make sense to start other churches that will also be weak."

These statements reveal a dangerous attitude. Strengthening existing work is imperative. If, however, a group purposely curtails growth in order to consolidate, the result is most often neither consolidation nor growth. Again Tippett says, "When the Spirit of God indicates the flood tide, that tide should be used to the full."[15] Growth as better should never supplant nor be supplanted by growth as bigger. The two must remain in balance.

Growing bigger and growing better are both valid and necessary parts of church growth. They must be in balance. There is, however, a third aspect to balanced growth, growing broader.

Growing Broader

Churches grow broader by ministry and missions. As a church or denomination reaches outside its own membership to meet the needs and relieve the suffering of persons in the community and the world, that church (or Church) is growing broader. As a church directly and indirectly (through mission giving) shares the gospel message in word and deed with other racial, national, or social groupings, that church is growing broader.

As a church meets its rightful responsibility in sharing the complete gospel with the entire world, that church is growing broader.

Social service is a vital part of the gospel and therefore an integral part of the Church's mission. Any religious group that follows the example of Jesus will naturally seek to meet the physical and social needs (see Luke 4:1-4). To participate in social involvement is neither "liberal" nor non-evangelistic. Actually, to refuse social involvement is to preach and practice a mutilated gospel.

One of the most welcome corrections in the teachings of the Church Growth Movement is found in C. Peter Wagner's *Church Growth and the Whole Gospel.* In this book Wagner admits to questioning the place of social action in a previous work. Wagner expresses his new conviction that while evangelism must remain the priority, there is also a cultural mandate and this mandate is a vital part of God's plan for his churches.[16] Wagner, in this statement, comes into line with two other evangelical writers, Carl F. H. Henry and David Moberg, who call for evangelical churches to recapture the social implications of the Bible and church ministry.[17]

Social involvement can take two forms. Social ministry seeks to care for those injured by society and circumstances. Using social ministry, a church feeds the hungry, gives clothing to the needy, provides care to sick and distressed, and comforts the mourning. Benevolence, though more often mentioned than done, is a part of the ministry of most churches.

A second type of social involvement, social action, seeks to change the structures of injustice and greed that bring the injury and suffering to mankind. Social action usually requires economic and political involvement. It may require courageous stands on controversial issues. It will doubtless open the church to charges of getting mixed up in things not spiritual. The Church and the churches must engage in social action. The prophets of God met injustice head on and demanded change (Amos 5:24). Churches can do no less.

To decry social involvement on the grounds of seeking numerical growth denys biblical Christianity. Nowhere is balance more necessary than in the relationship between evangelism, discipling, and social action. Evangelism and social ministry go hand-in-hand. If social efforts eclipse or take the place of evangelism, error has entered. If social effort is left out of the church program, the program is incomplete.

Conclusion

Churches must grow bigger, better, and broader. The health and ministry of the church depends on the presence of all three in proper balance. The question naturally arises as to how to know what the proper balance actually is. There is not, as you probably guessed, a set answer to this important question. The needs will vary from situation to situation. Evangelism always is the priority function of a church. There might be times of physical disaster when a church would feel the necessity to concentrate for a time on social services. This concentration would be temporary and as the physical needs declined, the church would return to a priority on evangelism.

At a time when the Spirit is granting evangelistic results, the harvest should be quickly gathered. If the harvest, of itself begins to wane, then more effort might be put into quality growth. When evangelistic results lag, the church might look to quality growth to train and motivate members to evangelism to the end that growing better would lead directly to growing bigger.

Balance has been lacking in some Church Growth thinking. The reasons for the emphasis on numerical growth have been explained. Balance is needed in church growth strategy and teaching. Achieving and maintaining proper balance is perhaps the most demanding and challenging task both for Church Growth teachers and for church leaders in the field.

Effective Evangelism

A third church growth basic, effective evangelism, should lie at the heart of the ministry of every church and every denomination. Effective evangelism means proclaiming by word and deed that Jesus Christ is God and Savior to the end that men and women accept him, become his disciples (followers), and responsible members of one of his churches. To be effective, evangelism must complete this entire cycle. The goal of effective evangelism is responsible, reproducing disciples of Jesus in responsible, reproducing congregations.

The phrase "disciple of Jesus" expresses the truth that effective evangelism seeks to bring persons to a relationship with Christ and thereby into personal discipleship for him. Effective evangelism seeks disciples rather than just decisions. Effective evangelism goes beyond the decision level attempting to be certain the person becomes a disciple.

A responsible disciple is one who does what is required and expected of a follower. He or she lives the Christian life. Responsible disciples pray, give, serve, witness, and grow. Responsible disciples carry out the Lord's will, meet the needs of mankind, and fulfill the ministry of his churches. Responsible disciples continue in the Lord's way, the Lord's teaching, and the Lord's work.

A responsible disciple is a reproducing disciple. Christians reproduce by leading others to discipleship. To fail at this point is to omit a crucial element in the Christian life. Effective evangelism leads believers to reproduce themselves in other believers through personal witness.

Effective evangelism motivates believers toward church membership. Until a believer becomes a responsible member of a church, evangelism has not reached its final goal. The goal is a responsible, reproducing believer in a church.

Effective evangelism desires and demands responsible, reproducing churches and expects to work with the congregations to help them become both responsible and reproducing. As a responsible disciple does those things expected of a disciple, so a responsible church does those things expected of a church. A responsible church worships, studies, serves, comforts, ministers, evangelizes, and engages in missionary activities. Churches, like disciples, must be responsible to the Lord of the Harvest.

A responsible church is a reproducing church. Disciples reproduce by producing (through the Spirit) another disciple. Churches reproduce by producing (also by the Spirit) another church. The new church may be accomplished directly by sponsoring a mission or it may be by missionary giving, praying, and cooperative effort. In whatever way or ways, a responsible church reproduces itself.

Church growth supports the concept of effective evangelism. Effective evangelism includes at least five facets: presence, proclamation, persuasion, perfecting, and participation in church membership.

Presence means contact. Lost people no longer come to the churches in large numbers. In third world areas, the lost are often unconscious or even antagonistic toward the presence of churches and unaffected by the preaching of the gospel. In both cases, if the lost are to be won, the gospel must be taken to them. Believers must initiate and maintain sympathetic contact with those who need the message of Jesus. Gospel-ready people must be sought. Contact with gospel-needy people must be continued. Presence, then, is a starting place for effective evangelism and some Christians fail at soul-winning because of lack of meaningful contact with the lost.

To be effective, however, evangelism must move beyond mere presence. The term *presence,* for some missiologists has come to mean an evangelistic strategy of contact, empathy, involvement, and reapproachment to those of other religions. Mission is seen as just being there. Presence, in these circles, means listening and respecting with little or no emphasis on conversion, the soft sell. Presence strategy centers on dialogue rather than proclamation.

Effective evangelism knows that simply being there is not enough. Listening and dialogue are important but only as they relate to witness. To be effective, evangelism must move beyond presence to proclamation.

Proclamation, the second facet of effective evangelism, means communication. The message of Jesus is to be shared not simply announced. The point of communicating the gospel is securing a response to God—not simply a hearing. The effective evangelist seeks to communicate God's message by word and deed to the end that the receptors come into a living relationship with the living God.

Genuine communication may be different from either preaching or verbal witnessing. These methods can at times effect only a hearing not a response. Communication takes place when the receptor comprehends the message in a personal way.

In Christian communication all efforts at impressing the hearers for the sake of the communicator must be laid aside. Charles Kraft insightfully says that

> when a vehicle of communication calls attention to itself, the message is lost. If, therefore, in a situation such as the preaching, singing, or organ playing situation, we become more aware of the performer's ability to perform than of the message he is seeking to get across, then the situation becomes a performance rather than a communication.[18]

Effective evangelism goes beyond contact to communication. Evangelism that stops at presence fails. Should the evangelist be satisfied with winning a hearing without personal response to the Person of the message, the evangelism will be ineffective. Effective evangelism, however, also refuses to stop at proclamation but goes on to the facet of persuasion.

Persuasion means conversion. The effective evangelist never uses methods that manipulate or coerce. One researcher found that people who felt manipulated in the decision to enter a church were 85 percent more likely to drop out of the church than those who entered without feeling manipulated.[19] Manipulation is not the meaning of persuasion.

While rejecting manipulative methods, the effective evangelist makes a definite effort to bring the lost person to a decision to accept Christ. Persuasion involves seeking commitment from the lost which leads to conversion. Some evangelistic methods lose effectiveness because evangelists feel that once a decision is made the work is finished. Hence, effort stops at persuasion or decision. Herein lies a danger in some evangelistic programs. One church found that of four pages of names of those who had made decisions in their homes only four could be found who had become church members. Effective evangelism moves beyond persuasion to perfecting.

Perfecting, the fourth facet of effective evangelism, means completing. The new believer must learn the ways of the faith and reach toward maturity in the faith. After birth, we expect a baby to grow. Effective evangelism is equally concerned with the process of growth and development (completing or perfecting) as with the act of converting.

An overemphasis on numbers for numbers' sake can lead to a concentration on decisions rather than disciples. Any evangelistic method that stops before providing for the spiritual nurture of the converts has failed to incorporate all phases of effective evangelism. Effective evangelism, then, proceeds from presence, to proclamation, to persuasion, to perfecting. But effective evangelism also moves on to the fifth facet, that is, participation in church membership.

Participation in church membership, or congregationalizing must become a part of all effective programs of evangelism. Evangelism has not completed its task until the believer is a responsible member of a responsible church. To be judged effective, evangelism must persist until the believer has become a working part of a living church.

To have an effective program of evangelism, a church or denomination must carefully plan to cover every facet of evangelism. To stop short at any point is to sacrifice evangelistic effectiveness. Every church and missionary organization must recognize the need of and provide for a full-faceted program of evangelism.

Some well-known and splendid missionary groups fall into the mistake of stopping short of a full-faceted program of evangelism. Some do a fine job of proclamation but fail to stress decision. Others properly emphasize decisions but do not reach the level of perfecting. Some groups even have beautiful programs that go through perfecting but stop short of providing for church membership. Effective evangelism must continue until every facet of evangelism has been reached. Only then can evangelism be said to be truly effective.

Church growth emphasizes evangelism but is only satisfied with effective evangelism. The charge that church growth is concerned only with the numerical increase of churches is unfounded. Effective evangelism, which provides for all five facets, is the only evangelism approved by church growth strategy.

The Unlimited Multiplication of Congregations

A fourth basic in church growth thinking is the unlimited multiplication of churches. There can be no effective expansion of the Christian movement apart from the creation of congregations where believers are incorporated. Local churches or fellowships provide the places in which people most naturally accept Christ, are nurtured in the faith, and find opportunities of service in the world. Planting growing churches of developing Christians was obviously the apostle Paul's method and must remain the primary method of Christian groups today.

Any missionary group that neglects the church planting aspect of missionary work creates a void that must either be filled by other groups or will result in inadequate Christian advance. To fulfill the Great Commission and make disciples of all peoples, a group must provide for the unlimited multiplication of local churches.

The Necessity of Churches

New congregations constitute a primary strategy in church growth planning. Donald A. McGavran emphasizes the primacy of local churches in God's redemptive program saying,

> What the fantastically mounting population of this world needs is fantastically multiplying churches which will enable liberated populations, filled with the Holy Spirit, to generate their own Calvins, Wesleys, Wilberforces and Martin Luther Kings, and their own sober, godly and fruitful societies.[20]

Jack Redford astutely points out that the church that does not accept church planting as a normal, natural function, has become "rootbound."[21] He sees church planting as the task of the local churches. In the same spirit, Timothy Starr declares church planting "always in season."[22]

In the United States and other nations, a major part of missionary endeavor must center on the planting of growing, reproducible, and reproducing churches. This emphasis on new churches, far from indicating any imperialistic tendency on the part of the planting group, only reveals the group's dedication to genuine, lasting, Christian advance. The ongoing development of a Christian movement demands a commitment to the unlimited multiplication of new Christian fellowships.

Objections to New Churches

Objections to the call for unlimited multiplication of new churches can be heard. For example, a series of articles in *The International Review of Missions,* July 1968, calls into question the stress McGavran had given to the need for new churches in his article, "Wrong Strategy: The Real Crisis in Mission."[23] Most workers who are committed to new congregations have met opposition to planting new churches.

One objection to new churches is the familiar refrain, "We already have too many churches." Increasing churches, goes the argument, will only lead to competition for members and less overall growth. While some areas may have less need for churches for the same kinds of people, even in those areas a need exists for churches for other groups. It constitutes unfaithfulness to the Lord and poor missionary strategy to limit new churches by any such rule as no new church can be planted within two miles of an existing congregation. There could be a need for multiple congregations in a two-mile area.

In one city in the United States, Win Arn heard local leaders declaring that sufficient churches already existed. That afternoon he called every church in the city and found the capacity of their worship centers. He discovered that if every church held three packed services each Sunday, there still would be insufficient space for all the people in the city.[24]

Another objection to new churches is stated, "We need to improve what we have before we create new churches." "After all," they say, "we have many weak churches that need help now. Why start more? Better to help these struggling churches than to start more that will likewise struggle."

This objection is understandable. Struggling churches do need help and should be helped. The needs of existing churches should not, however, deter a group from the constant multiplication of new congregations. Some churches continue to struggle because they are not willing to pay the price to grow or because they have internal problems. The cause of the Kingdom must take precedence over the needs of any smaller part of the body. The needs of existing churches must never impede the planting of new churches.

A third objection relates to the perceived inability to properly shepherd or provide leadership for new congregations. Fear is often expressed that to expand too rapidly might prevent proper supervision and lead to the formation of doctrinal or ethical unsoundness.

The apostle Paul did not share such concern. He planted churches widely and depended primarily on the Holy Spirit and minimum guidance to shepherd them. Melvin Hodges points out that the indigenous strategy of Paul allowed the planting of churches that were led by local leaders commissioned by the apostle. Paul himself remained only relatively brief periods in each place. He never saw a shortage of workers limiting the possibility for starting new churches.[25]

Roland Allen, in his well-known work on mission strategy, *Missionary Methods: St. Paul's Or Ours,* contends that Paul's method can still be used today. He rejects the idea that Paul lived in an exceptional day or was a man with resources unavailable to missionaries today. Allen is convinced that modern missionaries can and should employ Paul's strategy.[26] That strategy calls for the unlimited multiplication of churches.

Unlimited multiplication of churches at times leads to some difficulties and perhaps even unfortunate results. There may be doctrinal and ethical problems. Developments may take directions not intended or totally approved by the missionary. Some congregations will begin and die. The missionaries may have less control over the movement than they desire. In spite of such difficulties, it is imperative that for the good of the Kingdom, churches be planted everywhere.

Objections to church planting there are. Valid objections, however, are few. In almost every case, objections to new churches can be answered and the difficulties avoided. Missions must accept the continuing need for new congregations.

The Possibility of Diversity

The concept of the unlimited multiplication of churches is closely tied to the truth that churches can and should exist in a diversity of forms and use a diversity of methods. Every church must conform to biblical teachings as to the nature and function of a church. There can be, however, a remarkable and beautiful diversity of methods, worship style, etc. in churches which all remain faithful to the biblical images of a church.

A denomination must rid itself of the idea that a church must conform to some traditional pattern in organization, practice, or method. Too often, a church that uses different methods or does things in nontraditional ways is not accepted by the denominational machinery. Many of the traditional requirements are just that, traditional, rather than biblical. So long as a church conforms to the biblical images of a church, that church should not only be allowed but encouraged in its efforts.

A church may be large or small. It may meet in special buildings or use rented quarters. It may follow traditional patterns in worship, music, and ministry or it may use radically different approaches. It may have full-time or bivocational leadership. The important factor is that the church be biblical. So long as it is biblical, diversity is an advantage rather than a problem.

Interestingly, sometimes the "different" congregations are more biblical than the more traditional churches. Church growth can be obstructed when churches are forbidden to express their nature because of loyalty to denominational tradition. Diversity in types of churches is a basic need in church growth planning.

This is no plea for letting down doctrinal standards. To fully explain what I am saying, we need to look at the Bible and see what are the biblical images of a church. When a church lives up to these images, diversity is allowable. For example, a particular church exhibits a church-as-usual, traditional approach. The highly trained, skilled, full-time staff accomplishes most of the ministry functions and leads the well-organized, formal worship services. The membership primarily sits, watches, and follows.

Another church insists that every member is a minister. Every member is expected to discover and use in the church program his/her spiritual gifts. The church meets in rented quarters for the once-a-week celebration. Other activities take place in home fellowship groups. The church is led by a husband-wife team who serve as co-pastors. Recently the church asked a lady (not the pastor's wife) to baptize a woman convert in whose conversion experience the lady had been instrumental.

Obviously, the first church is traditional—the second is not. The call for diversity is a call to recognize and encourage both churches. Both conform to biblical images of a church. If either falls short of the biblical pattern it would be the first church rather than the second. As Jerry Wafford and Kenneth Kilinski say,

> The church of today is failing to fulfill its purpose largely because it has ceased to be an organism. A church in which one person preaches, a few teach, and a few others work in an administrative ministry, but the vast majority simply listen, learn, and follow without becoming functioning members of the body, is not an integrated organism.[27]

Evangelizing and congregationalizing this world demands a diversity of types of churches. Some will use different music, be more emotional, employ varying methods of worship and ministry. In order to reach all people let us encourage a diversity of churches and not seek to force every congregation into a set pattern of worship and ministry.

Conclusion

Church growth is convinced that the Kingdom and the churches grow most effectively through the planting and developing of many new congregations. As the churches in the New Testament period multiplied, so must churches today. The mounting populations of the world call for a vast planting of churches in order that these peoples might be reached. The multiplication of churches is one of the basics of church growth.

Reliance on the Holy Spirit

No strategy produces growth in God's churches. Only the power of the Holy Spirit can produce the spiritual harvest that alone is acceptable to God and therefore to the followers of church growth. Church growth never seeks to replace the Holy Spirit with any dependence on method. Church growth teaches that the Spirit is active in revealing where the message should be shared, how it should be shared, and in giving the harvest upon the sharing. This is to say that even the strategies themselves must come from the Spirit. Church growth, therefore, from the beginning to the end, relies totally on the Holy Spirit.

Questions and Activities

1. List the relationships you have with others that might serve as "bridges of God."
2. What is a "responsible believer" and a "responsible church"? How does the concept of reproducibility relate to responsibility?
3. How many churches does an area need?
4. Study your church's record. What is the relationship between the number of people baptized and the number who continue actively engaged in church ministry? Do you think your church's growth is balanced? Does your church need more emphasis on growing bigger? or better? or broader?

Further Reading

Getz, Gene. *Sharpening the Focus of the Church* (Moody)
Chaney, Charles L. and Lewis, Ron S., *Design for Church Growth* (Broadman)
Thompson, Oscar, *Concentric Circles of Concern* (Broadman)
McDill, Wayne, *Making Friends for Christ* (Broadman)
McGavran, Donald A. and Hunter, George III, *Church Growth Strategies that Work* (Abingdon)
Wagner, C. Peter, *The Crest of the Wave* (Regal)

Notes

1. Donald A. McGavran and George G. Hunter III, *Church Growth Strategies that Work* (Nashville: Abingdon Press, 1980), pp. 28-29.
2. Ibid., p. 30.
3. Ibid., p. 34
4. Ebbie C. Smith, *God's Miracles: Indonesian Church Growth* (South Pasadena, Calif.: William Carey Library, 1970), pp. 98-101.
5. Orlando E. Costas, *The Integrity of Mission* (San Francisco: Harper and Row, Publishers, 1979), pp. 37-60 reflects something of this idea, saying churches should grow in breadth, depth, and height. See also Delos Miles, *Church Growth—A Mighty River* (Nashville: Broadman Press), p. 148.
6. Smith, pp. 94-96.
7. Ibid., pp. 80-82.
8. McGavran, *Understanding Church Growth,* pp. 11-12.
9. Charles L. Chaney, *Church Planting at the End of the Twentieth Century* (Wheaton, Ill.: Tyndale House Publishing, Inc., 1982), pp. 39-58.
10. Alan R. Tippett, *Church Growth and the Word of God* (Grand Rapids: Wm. B. Eerdmans Publishing Co., 1970), p. 16.
11. C. Peter Wagner, *Your Church Can Grow* (Glendale, Calif.: Regal Books, 1976), pp. 22-25,52-54.
12. Philip Barron Jones, "an Examination of the Statistical Growth of the Southern Baptist Convention," in *Understanding Church Growth and Decline: 1950-1978* ed. Dean R. Hoge and David A. Roozen (New York: The Pilgrim Press, 1979), p. 172.
13. Ibid.
14. Alan R. Tippett, *Verdict Theology in Missionary Theory* (Lincoln, Ill.: Lincoln Christian College Press, 1969), p. 127.
16. C. Peter Wagner, *Church Growth and the Whole Gospel* (San Francisco: Harper and Row, Publishers, 1981), pp. xi-xiii, 12-14,33-42.
17. Carl F. H. Henry, *A Plea for Evangelical Demonstration* (Grand Rapids: Wm. B. Eerdmans, 1971); *The Uneasy Conscience of Modern Fundamentalism* (Grand Rapids: Wm. B. Eerdmans, 1947); David Moberg, *The Great Reversal* (New York: J. B. Lippincott Co., 1972).

18. Charles Kraft, *Communicating the Gospel God's Way* (South Pasadena, Calif.: William Carey Library, 1979), p. 5.

19. Flavil R. Yeakly, Jr., *Why Churches Grow* (Broken Arrow, Okla.: Christian Communications, Inc., 1979), pp. 53-58.

20. Donald A. McGavran, "Wrong Strategy: The Real Crisis in Mission," *The International Review of Missions* 54 (1965):451-61.

21. Jack Redford, *Planting New Churches* (Nashville: Broadman Press, 1978), p. 23.

22. Timothy Starr, *Church Planting: Always in Season* (Toronto, Canada: Fellowship of Evangelical Baptist Churches in Canada, 1978), pp. 33,193,195.

23. McGavran, "Wrong Strategy," pp. 451-61.

24. McGavran and Hunter, p. 103.

25. Melvin L. Hodges, *The Indigenous Church* (Springfield, Mo.: Gospel Publishing House, 1953), pp. 3-4.

26. Roland Allen, *Missionary Methods: St. Paul's or Ours?* (Grand Rapids: Wm. B. Eerdmans Publishing Co., 1962), pp. 151-63.

27. Jerry Wafford and Kenneth Kilinski, *Organization and Leadership in the Local Church* (Grand Rapids: Zondervan, 1973), p. 134.

3
Testing Strategies for Church Growth

A vast number of strategies or methods exist which under various circumstances lead to church growth. While acknowledging the existence of hundreds of strategies, the Church Growth Movement does not approve of all methods. As seen earlier, only those strategies that are compatible with biblical teachings and that produce biblically approved results are judged by Church Growth to be acceptable.

This chapter suggests how strategies can be tested to ascertain their appropriateness. To this end, we will look at some of the more often challenged of the strategies suggested by Church Growth and question their validity. The strategies in question relate to the homogeneous unit, the indigenous church, the people movement, and discipling then perfecting.

The Foundation and the Superstructure

Before turning to specific strategies, let us establish that valid church growth is built on a theological foundation. The methods, which are what most people hear of church growth, are the superstructure built on this foundation. Failure to understand this truth can distort the understanding of church growth.

Church growth concepts promote building solidly on the theological foundation of a loving, seeking, finding God; the dying, resurrected, redeeming Christ; needy, unbelieving, perishing mankind; full, free salvation for repentant persons in Jesus; and a responding, sharing church. Church Growth teaches that preaching the gospel to every person (Great Commission) constitutes the basic purpose of the Church.

Biblical theology, then, provides the foundation for church growth. Most of what Church Growth writers speak, however, relates to strategy and methods. The foundation is not continuously restated but is ever present. Church Growth theory is primarily a body of teaching related to methods by which churches can grow.

Because Church Growth Theory is composed of both a theological foundation and a methodological superstructure, persons of various theological persuasions can embrace together the strategy portion. This is not to say that any theological position is suitable for church growth strategy or that church growth strategy is compatible with every theological persuasion. Only those who accept the validity of Great Commission missions are likely to approve of and be attracted by church growth strategies. Yet, Christians and groups with varying views of the millenium, differing ideas of the manner of baptism and church government, and opposing concepts of the meaning of God's sovereignty could all accept and employ Church Growth methods. There is "a" theology for church growth but not "the" theology.

As every theology is not suitable for church growth, so every strategy is not approved. More than a positive answer to the question, "Does it work?" is necessary for a strategy to be acceptable. Church growth does not and must not accept the idea that the end (growth) justifies any means. Every strategy must be tested.

Testing of both the theological foundation and the methodological superstructure is imperative. The standard in both cases is the Bible—both in its direct teaching and its underlying principles. How do biblical teachings relate to the strategies of church growth?

The Homogeneous Unit Strategy in the Perspective of Christian Ethics and Responsive Evangelism

The homogeneous unit strategy (gathering people of similar social, educational, or economic levels into one church) remains the most often discussed and least understood aspect of Church Growth theory. Major concerns are voiced regarding the theological and ethical implications of churches built on homogeneous lines. Questions heard are, "Are homogeneous churches soundly Christian?" "Do such churches provide for genuine attainment of Christian brotherhood and fellowship?" "Is it theologically and ethically proper to emphasize the separateness of mankind rather than to seek oneness and brotherhood in Christ?"

These are important questions. Church growth advocates cannot and should not ignore them. Followers of church growth must subject the homogeneous strategy to vigorous and honest scrutiny.

The Strategy Explained

The homogeneous unit (hereafter referred to as HU) strategy is one method of evangelizing and congregationalizing persons from the diverse groupings (cultures) of the world by providing congregations into which they can be gathered so as to allow them to consider the invitation to salvation without unnecessarily leaving their own people or forcing them into customs and practices either foreign to or unacceptable to their life-styles and backgrounds. This is an involved definition. Amplifying its meaning will help.

A Strategy Not a Principle

Confusion has arisen over the term, "homogeneous principle." I consider the homogeneous approach to be a strategy rather than a rule or principle. I am uncomfortable with Peter Wagner's concept that the homogeneous unit approach is the nearest thing to a law in Church Growth thinking.[1] This makes the HU approach a principle. Principles are absolute; they stand for what should be everywhere at all times. For example, "God's ideal for marriage is one man and one woman for life in a one-flesh relationship," is biblical principle. Although never completely reached, it remains God's principle for marriage.

A strategy, in contrast to a principle, is a means to an end. Strategies can be altered or set aside as situations demand. Strategies are methods used to reach goals set by principles. The homogeneous unit strategy does not teach that all churches must or should be for a particular group of people. It does approve of beginning churches targeted for a particular group in order to more effectively evangelize them.

In Church Growth thinking the absolutes are the theological truths concerning salvation and God's desire for growing churches. The rest of church growth is methodology and can, therefore, be used or set aside as circumstances demand.

The homogeneous unit strategy has proved effective in reaching individuals and groups with the gospel. The failure to employ the strategy has proved detrimental to effective, responsive evangelism and church planting. The HU strategy is one, but only one method of evangelizing and congregationalizing the world's population.

The Plurality of Mankind

The homogeneous unit concept recognizes and accepts the plurality or diversity of mankind. This pluralism stands as an easily recognized and incontestable fact in human society. Wagner suggests that the pluralism among mankind is in keeping with God's plan and in mankind's best interests.[2] In line with this concept, Church Growth does not decry the diversity that exists in societies.

Unquestionably, injustice, prejudices, and tragic discrimination have grown out of the plurality of mankind. Abuses associated with pluralism are to be decried; the injustices and evils done in its name righted. There are, however, positive aspects to pluralism. The differences in peoples and cultures adds to the interchange of ideas and discoveries and thus to the flavor of existence.

Peoples (cultures, groupings, tribes, language entities, occupational groups, etc.) of the world form what Donald A. McGavran calls the mosaic of mankind.[3] Each piece in the mosaic adds its own color, texture, and shape to the whole. The whole is incomplete without the pieces and the pieces of less beauty until seen as parts of the whole. Recognizing both the reality and positive nature of the mosaic concept, church growth seeks, not to create nor even perpetuate divisions, but simply works with the groupings of mankind as they exist.

The HU strategy does not intend and should never be used to amplify or rationalize racism. Race, as a matter of fact, becomes less and less central to homogeneous units in modern society. The mosaic is based on many factors, only one of which is race. Factors such as occupation, education, age, special interests, and background draw people into homogeneous units. A homogeneous unit today is often composed of people from various racial backgrounds. The charge brought by Ralph Elliott, that church growth seeks to produce segregated, racist churches, is nothing short of myth.[4] HUs are not synonomous with race in today's world.

Homogeneous units are, then, segments of a population in which members have some characteristics in common. It is an elastic concept, more clearly defined and understood in the context in which it is used. Edward R. Dayton, in *Unreached Peoples 80,* defines a HU as, "A significantly large sociological grouping of individuals who perceive themselves to have a common affinity for one another."[5] Perhaps this definition should include something of a willingness or even predisposition to follow the direction of the group.

Church Growth teaches that evangelism is more effective when congregations provide for the differing values and practices of people so they can come to Christ and into his church without leaving their own people. McGavran's often quoted statement, "Men like to become Christians without crossing racial, linguistic, or class barriers," has led to extensive discussion.[6] Reacting to the statement, Francis M. DuBose says that "no man establishes the terms on which he will receive the gospel—the gospel establishes its own terms."[7] What DuBose hears in McGavran's statement is not, of course, what McGavran said. There is no question in McGavran's mind, or in the mind of other Church Growth writers, that salvation comes only by personal faith in Christ and that every person must respond to the demands of repentance and faith. McGavran has written:

> Church growth is basically a theological stance. God requires it. It looks to the Bible for direction as to what God wants done. It believes that Acts 4:12, John 14:6, and scores of similar passages are true. It holds that belief in Jesus Christ, understood according to the Scriptures, is necessary for salvation. Church growth rises in unshakeable theological conviction.[8]

Church Growth knows that the basis of salvation is theological not social.

When McGavran says that the great obstacles for conversion are social, not theological, he is not, as Larry L. McSwain claims, emphasizing sociology as the medium for understanding conversion.[9] The point is that social and family factors construct barriers that restrict many from considering the gospel. Because of these social barriers they remain deaf to the message. Church Growth does not seek to wipe out the scandal of the cross. Using the HU strategy, Church Growth seeks to provide congregations which do not place unnecessary or artificial barriers in the way of persons who should consider Christ. The existence of homogeneous unit churches does not erase the necessity of theological decision, it only opens the way for it.

The point can be seen in the history of evangelism in Andra Pradesh Province in India. The missionaries began work in the late 1800s among the upper castes and experienced virtual rejection of the message. Using good strategy, the missionaries turned to the then responsive "outcastes" and a church was founded. The work went so well that soon church leadership was placed in the hands of the national leaders. Between 1928-1933 a movement to Christ began among the Shudras, a lower caste people. The outcastes saw no reasons to form new churches for these Shudras. "They can come to our churches," they said. The failure to provide churches into which the Shudras could naturally flow without crossing caste barriers inhibited the movement among the Shudras.[10] A more viable strategy would have been to plant churches patterned for the Shudras into which they could naturally flow.

Not an Ultimate Strategy

The homogeneous unit concept is not the ultimate strategy. The ultimate expression of the Kingdom of God is a classless, casteless society of brotherhood. Plurality may remain but fellowship will be unbroken. The HU strategy is one step on the way to the development of the final Church. Some misunderstanding can be averted if: Church Growth Writers are heard on the matter of homogeneous unit churches. McGavran has said,

> In applying this principle, common sense must be assumed. The creation of narrow Churches, selfishly centered on the salvation of their own kith and kin only, is never the goal. Becoming Christian should never enhance animosities or the arrogance which is so common to all human associations. As men of one class, tribe, or society come to Christ, the Church will seek to moderate their ethnocentrism in many ways. She will teach them that persons from other segments of society are also God's children. God so loved the world, she will say, that He gave His only Son that *whosoever* believes in Him might have eternal life. She will educate leaders of several homogeneous unit Churches in one training school. She will work with the great current in human affairs which is leading on to a universal culture. She will make sure that her people are in the vanguard of brotherly practices. The one thing she will *not* do—on the basis that it is self-defeating—is to substitute kindness and friendliness for the Gospel. She knows that the first is the fruit and the second the root.
>
> And the Church, I am sure, will not deify the principle I am describing in this chapter, whether it brings men into the Way or not. Knowing that growth is a most complex process, she will humbly recognize that God uses many factors as yet not understood by us, and will not insist that He use just this one. If in a given instance, congregations which neglect this principle grow better than those which observe it, she will not blindly follow the principle. She will be open to the leading of the Holy Spirit.
>
> The Church will remember that many factors contribute to church growth and a suitable combination is more important than any one factor. She will not press the factor emphasized in this chapter disproportionately nor allow it to obscure others. Good judgment and a humble dependence on God who alone gives growth is assumed in this discussion.
>
> The Homogeneous Unit Principle is certainly not the heart of church growth,

> but has nevertheless great applicability to many situations in America and other lands all around the world. Apply with common sense is the rule.[11]

Here then is the point, churches will be targeted to a particular group of people to aid in their evangelization. After these people are brought into the Kingdom and into a church, continued growth in Christian living will break down the social barriers to brotherhood. The church will strive to bridge to other groups as it continues to grow. The HU strategy is primarily a strategy for the beginning evangelistic stage and is not to be a permanent part of the life of the church.

It is true that many churches will remain largely class or group congregations and will serve primarily a specific group. This is not particularly bad so long as we avoid the idea that churches are supposed to be this way and the mistake of basing segregation on the concept. As T. B. Maston, Professor of Christian Ethics, has said:

> Furthermore, the people to whom the church ministers come from differing cultural background; they represent varying educational levels and vocational interests. Their outlook on life may differ widely. These things determine largely their choice of associates and their relations with others. This carries over to their church. Even different types of religious services appeal to people with varying backgrounds. For example, the socially and economically underprivileged express their religion more in emotional terms than those of the middle and upper classes. Most of them would not feel at home in a beautifully ornate church building, nor in a more or less formal type of worship service. . . . Whether we like it or not, it seems that we shall continue to have class churches. This is not particularly bad if there is retained a spirit of Christian fellowship between the churches of different classes. It will be most unfortunate, however, if there arises a hierarchy of class among the churches; if denominational leaders and agencies give special recognition or preferment to the churches of any particular class or to the pastors and leaders of those churches.[12]

As a beginning strategy the HU approach is both effective and acceptable. The church which begins as a homogeneous unit congregation as it develops will reach out to more and more kinds of people and become less and less a one-people church.

The Strategy Examined

Many accept the HU strategy as a viable method of missionary work. Others, however, question the approach. If the HU strategy is to have widespread acceptance it must be correctly understood. The strategy must, therefore, be examined by considering a series of questions.

1. Does the homogeneous unit strategy produce numerical and organic (quality) growth in Christians and churches? The answer is yes. Even those who question the strategy often admit it works. In fact, it has been said that the fact it works is the worst thing about it.

McGavran notes the Congregacao Cristan in Brazil as an example of the working of the HU strategy. This Church, made up originally of Italian immigrants, grew from a few in 1916 to over 260,000 in 1962. Of this movement McGavran says,

> None can imagine that the Congregacao has grown among a primitive people. Yet here, too, the principle that men like to become Christians without crossing class and language barriers is clearly a factor in the amazing growth. It must be emphasized that in Sao Paulo, during the years 1910 to 1962, the Methodists, Baptists, Lutherans, and Presbyterians were strong. Only a very small number of the responsive Italians, however, became Evangelicals in these well-established, Portuguese-speaking denominations, each with notable mission schools and colleges buttressing it. Among other reasons, unquestionably one was this: that to become Evangelicals in any of these four Churches, Italians would have had to cross linguistic and class barriers and leave their own community. This Brazilian illustration has great meaning in the United States, where until indigenous movements within each minority surge ahead, great growth is unlikely.[13]

A different strategy with far less results was employed among the Quechuas of Ecuador. Missionaries sought to evangelize the Quechuas and incorporate them into the Spanish-speaking, Spanish-culture churches. Little harvest was realized so long as becoming Christian seemed to the Quechuas the same as becoming Spanish. McGavran notes that "it is easily proved that where significant numbers of Indians have turned to Evangelical faith, it is because a way has been found whereby they can become Evangelicals without leaving their own people."[14]

The HU strategy allows for numerical growth. It also promotes Christian growth as believers are incorporated into churches where they can be nurtured and provided with opportunities for service. Admittedly, care must be taken also to develop missionary fervor in the members of HU churches.

2. Does the homogeneous unit strategy produce or support racism, segregation, or isolationist churches? The plain answer is, it should not, but it may, and in some cases has done so. A danger in the HU approach lies

exactly at the point of it being used to support or even intensify separation between peoples.

Some will and have used the HU concept to excuse or defend racism and separation. Any such statement as, "Let them have their own churches and stay out of ours," reveals an unbiblical attitude, a sinful disposition, and a total misunderstanding of the homogeneous unit concept. A true church breaks down animosity and builds up love and fellowship between believers. The cross should break down the walls of hostility between peoples (Eph. 2:14-22) and where this does not happen, the cross is being denied its full working. Racism and segregation must never hide beneath the cloak of the HU strategy.

A balancing word needs to be said here. The danger of racist attitudes does not invalidate the HU strategy. After all, does anyone think such unchristian attitudes arise only in HU churches? To refuse to use the HU strategy is to demand that unsaved peoples come into churches which are made up of people different from them and which employ practices foreign to their experience. This is to ask the unsaved to incorporate the ethical dimensions of the gospel to a greater extent than do many Christians. To insist on conglomerate churches is to ask for the fruit of Christianity, brotherhood, before having the root, salvation. The HU strategy does not speak to existing churches and say, "You may remain homogeneous." It says to the lost, "We will plant churches for you to help remove the artificial barriers that may exist in your minds about entering the Faith and the church."

A second danger in the HU approach is that of leading to isolated, nonmissionary churches that consider their entire task that of ministering to our kind of people. This very problem can be seen in a HU Church, the Batak Church in Indonesia. Over one million Bataks are members of this Church. The Batak Church is almost totally a church for Bataks. Little effort to reach non-Bataks is visible.[15] The HU strategy should never be allowed to lower missionary zeal or activity.

No approach is free from all danger of misuse. When the HU strategy is used as an initial method which is followed by an active advance in brotherhood and missions, the dangers can be avoided. Any group employing the HU strategy must guard against the racist and isolationist possibilities.

3. Does the homogeneous strategy allow for an authentic church that fulfills both the evangelistic and the cultural mandates? The answer is, Yes.

Church Growth thinking emphasizes bridging, that is, the gospel moves from group to group just as it moves from person to person across relational lines. As a church expands to other groups it reaches not only the evangelistic mandate but the cultural mandate of promoting brotherhood as well. Moreover, as the church continues to grow, it should become aware of further social needs and expand its ability to respond to these needs.

Church Growth Theory in general increasingly accepts the necessity of responding to the cultural mandate and engaging in social ministry. The HU strategy in no way conflicts with a church meeting the cultural mandate. As the church continues to bridge it will accept its responsibility to become a church for all people.

4. Can the homogeneous pattern be seen in the New Testament? Yes, I think it can. All churches in the New Testament period, however, were not homogeneous unit churches. Some Church Growth Writers have tried too hard to find the principle in every New Testament record of churches. It is true that both Hellenistic Jews and Palestinian Jews were members of the Jerusalem Church. Had not the problem of slighting the Grecian widows arisen the need for deacons would not have been felt (see Acts 6:1-7). Further, the account of Philemon and Onesimus reveals the presence of both owner and slave in the same congregation.

It is well to remember in this regard that masters and slaves were considered part of the same household in New Testament times. Thus, the presence of slave and master in the same congregation would not be as unusual as it might appear to modern thinkers. Paul's efforts to begin at the Jewish synagogue and move to the "God-fearers" rather than a denial of HU thinking could be seen as a support of it. These "God-fearers" formed a group that already possessed strong ties to the Jewish community (see Acts 13:46-52). Furthermore, the Jerusalem council gave approval for churches more in keeping with Gentile culture (see Acts 15).

Some indication exists that the homogeneous strategy, while not the only or even the dominant pattern in the New Testament, was recognized and allowed. Paul Minear in *The Obedience of Faith,* suggests a diversity of congregations in Rome. Minear says:

> We should remember the great size of the city of Rome and its polyglot population, which included a large Jewish ghetto, a large number of satellite suburbs, and various neighborhoods which retained their own ethnic and cultural distinctiveness within the metropolitan area. Among the synagogues the variations in origin were often reflected: e.g., there were synagogues of the

> Asians, the Judeans, the Achaeans. Instead of visualizing a single Christian congregation, therefore, we should constantly reckon with the probability that within the urban area were to be found forms of Christian community which were as diverse, and probably also as alien, as the churches of Galatia and those of Judea. Consequently, the apostle was attempting within the bounds of a single letter to address them all. We must look very closely then at these various groups. I believe that we may distinguish at least five distinct factions, or if faction be too strong a word, five different positions.[16]

This view of the churches in Rome fits the HU pattern. Thus, the homogeneous strategy, while not the exclusive New Testament pattern, can be seen in the New Testament record. The important point is, however, that understood and used properly, the homogeneous unit strategy does not violate biblical standards for brotherhood and unity among believers.

5. Is it not possible that rejecting the homogeneous strategy might establish unnecessary barriers to the evangelization of some peoples and groups? This problem has been addressed previously and the answer is obviously, Yes. To insist, by failing to provide alternatives, that people come into churches incompatible with their culture and life-styles builds unnecessary barriers to their considering the gospel.

Paul rejected the Judaizers and their attempt to erect barriers to Gentile response through insistence on circumcision and other Jewish ritual. The HU strategy allows churches in which different groups can enjoy their kind of music, and worship services as well as being with people who talk like, dress like, and think like they do. These differences can be overcome among Christians (though not easily).

The HU strategy simply begs that unbelievers not be forced to leave their own people to become Christians. In order to be followers of Christ, people will have to reject some aspects of their own culture but do not have to reject their culture completely. The insistence that people must enter our kind of church and worship in our way may be more unethical than any movement toward homogeneous unit churches.

6. Is diversity, as expressed in the homogeneous unit strategy, a possibility for churches today? Again, Yes. Diversity is not wrong. I agree with Peter Wagner's assessment:

> In Christianity both unity and diversity are important values. Today's challenge to the churches, as I see it, is not to eliminate the diversity of the groups within the church. Rather, we are called to eliminate any fear, hostility, and conflict that such diversity might cause and, at the same time, to discover ways in which diversity can become a positive force producing richness, variety, and

> mutual appreciation among Christians. This challenge calls for a new theoretical basis upon which the necessary creative structures can be developed. My hypothesis for such a starting point is this: *the local congregation in a given community should be only as integrated as are the families and other primary social groups in the community, while intercongregational activities and relationships should be as integrated as are the secondary social groups in the community or society as a whole.*[17]

Upon examination, then, the homogeneous unit strategy meets biblical standards and is an acceptable option for evangelistic and congregationalizing work. It must, of course, be applied carefully. To fail to plant homogeneous unit churches erects unnecessary barriers to the gospel.

The Strategy Applied

The homogeneous strategy must be thoughtfully applied. The application of this strategy must be such as would not lead to nor reinforce unethical attitudes or unmissionary results. Few institutions are more strictly segregated than the middle class churches from which some critics decry the HU strategy. In applying this strategy, several guidelines should be followed.

1. Every church must be consciously open to all—in both membership and fellowship. No one should be excluded from any church. The HU strategy only seeks to establish churches that provide a more open opportunity for evangelism. Any church that purposely excludes other peoples is missing the point of Christian fellowship.

2. Maintain solidly a denominational heterogeneity. While local churches may at least to some degree remain homogeneous, a denomination should resist the temptation to move away from any grouping of peoples. Most denominations are missing great opportunities by not establishing churches among the very poor who may constitute the greatest mission field in the United States. A denomination should be wide enough to have churches for every group—ethnic, language, culture. A denomination should be wide enough to have churches of all sizes and types, ideally organized for all kinds of people.

3. Work tirelessly to overcome unchristian and unbiblical prejudices and hatreds. The church, of all places, should recognize the necessity of Christian brotherhood and mutual respect. Every effort to develop brotherhood must be expended. This effort will be exerted both within congregations and between congregations. The homogeneous strategy should enhance rather than destroy Christian brotherhood.

4. Study thoroughly the needs of every community. Churches and denominations should seek to know their communities so as to provide the congregations to reach every group of people. To insist on only one type of church and require it to be our type of church places unnecessary barriers or restraints on multitudes and delays the harvest. When unevangelized groups are found, they should be served immediately. Usually this is best accomplished through churches targeted directly to their group and in which they can feel comfortable.

Conclusion

The homogeneous unit strategy is an acceptable methodology. The concept holds promise of unusual effectiveness. To fail to use the strategy may well hinder the harvest. Christian groups should therefore, make full use of this important methodology, applying it creatively to reap the harvest intended by the Lord.

Indigenous Church Strategy

The concept of the indigenous church strategy, while less controversial than homogeneous unit strategy, still has generated considerable discussion and needs, therefore, to be tested. This strategy, which has gained widespread popularity among mission groups, contributes to church growth when correctly understood and applied. Testing will indicate, I think, that indigenous methods are valid, productive, and ethically acceptable for modern missionary strategy.

Understanding Indigenous Strategies

Like the homogeneous unit strategy, the indigenous church methodology is one method but not the only method of evangelizing and congregationalizing. Indigenous patterns can lay greater claim to universality than homogeneous patterns. All churches are not and need not be homogeneous. All churches (and Churches) will increase their effectiveness as they move toward more indigenous patterns.

The term *indigenous,* though often used, unfortunately, is not always clearly understood. The indigenous approach is sometimes equated with nationalization or turning the church over to the nationals. Others restrict the idea of indigenous strategy to self-support and feel that the elimination of outside financial aid will ensure an indigenous church. These and similar restrictions to the indigenous concept fail to clearly perceive and correctly express the total meaning of indigenous strategy.

William A. Smalley contributed significantly to the proper understanding of indigenous strategy in his definition of an indigenous church. He wrote:

> It [an indigenous church] is a group of believers who live out their life, including their socialized Christian activity, in the patterns of the local society, and for whom any transformation of that society comes out of their felt needs under the guidance of the Holy Spirit and the Scriptures.[18]

This definition expands the indigenous concept beyond the "three-self formula" made famous by Henry Venn, Rufus Anderson, John Nevius, Roland Allen, and in recent times by Melvin Hodges and Calvin Guy. The three selfs, "self-governing, self-supporting, and self-propagating," certainly contained truth concerning effective missionary strategy. Too often, attention centered on self-support or self-government alone and the wider meanings of an indigenous church were thus overlooked.

An indigenous church grows naturally and reproduces successfully in the culture of its members. Foreign domination ceases. Patterns incompatible with local ways are avoided. Change is effected by the people themselves under the leadership of the Holy Spirit. An indigenous church then, fits naturally into the culture of its people.

Indigenous strategy does not accommodate to the point that the church incorporates sin, evil, or injustice—no matter how cultural these may be. Obviously, a genuine church ever challenges the wrong and evil in culture. An indigenous church does, however, allow the expression of biblical truth to be in terms of the culture and thought forms of the people.

In an attempt to more accurately delineate the nature of an indigenous church, Allen R. Tippett points to six marks of an indigenous church. When taken together the marks contribute to the church's unique "self-hood."[19] One mark of an indigenous church is its self-image. The church sees itself as the Body of Christ in the local situation. It feels responsible for expressing Christ's love to the community. An indigenous church accepts itself as Christ's church and does not view itself as being dependent on or subject to an outside mission organization.

A second mark of an indigenous church is self-functioning. Such a church has the necessary parts, which working together, accomplish the various functions of the church. The church can provide for its own worship, study groups, training programs, and community ministries. Missionaries assist, but an indigenous church can function on its own abilities, facilities, and strengths.

A third mark of an indigenous church relates to the self-determining capacity. This church makes its own decisions in the pattern most natural to the cultural setting. Tippett says so well:

> The decision must be with the people themselves or their approved representative, not with an external authority like a mission or missionary. The only authority a missionary retains in a truly indigenous Church is the authority of the office to which the nationals appoint him. Then, the decision-making should be carried out within a structure which is culturally appropriate. It should reflect in some way the accepted decision-making mechanisms of the tribe; that is, it should be something they can feel is their own. The greatest threat to an indigenous Church is the denominational structures. Every missionary organization should be ready to fit the culture.[20]

Self-support is the fourth mark of an indigenous church. The indigenous church supports both its own financial needs and those of its service projects. Subsidy, the provision of financial and material needs from sources outside the congregation, has long constituted a major question for missionary strategy.

Subsidy can be defined as any material provision from outside the church (Church) that relieves the church itself from either support or responsibility. The mission agency that provides buildings and underwrites salary for church workers is using subsidy. The mission organization that pays for the training school or social service (hospitals, etc.) likewise is subsidizing.

Subsidy allows for partnership. It provides a means by which more affluent segments of the Church can assist less affluent or developed segments. When both segments are contributing according to ability and the giving segment does not demand or expect control, subsidy may be used with positive effect.

In most cases, subsidy produces negative rather than positive results. Subsidy does not always lead to dependence or paternalism, but these are the usual tendencies. Furthermore, subsidy puts a ceiling on outreach. If every new church or ministry must await financial backing from outside, a built-in limitation exists. Indigenous churches (and ministries) that can live, thrive, and reproduce in their own settings allow for unlimited expansion.

An indigenous church should be self-supporting. If any form of aid is employed, administrative decisions should rest with the church rather than the group giving the aid.

The fifth mark of an indigenous church, self-propagation, means a church reproduces itself in kind. Both evangelism and church planting are emphasized. Indigenous churches take responsibility for evangelizing their immediate region and for missionary effort in other regions. Such a church (Church) does not depend on others to reach new persons or areas.

The sixth mark of an indigenous church is the quality of self-giving. The needy in the area receive comfort, love, and physical help from an indigenous church. The service reaches not only to members of the church but to needy persons outside the membership as well.

Tippett has, with these marks, expanded the meaning of an indigenous church. When local Christians lead out and the church begins to meet these marks in its own strength, the church has moved toward indigenization.

Thus, an indigenous church means more than simply a self-supporting church or one in which the nationals have authority. Peter Wagner has summarized an indigenous church, which he chooses to call a maturing church, as one that can take care of itself, that is a church for others which is relevant to the cultural situation.[21]

Advantages of Indigenous Strategies

Pragmatism has been given as the primary reason for using indigenous strategies. These strategies seem to work better. They contribute to more rapid growth of churches. McGavran points not only to the popularity of indigenous strategies in present-day missions, but also mentions eight reasons why indigenous churches grow better.[22]

The fact that it works does not, in itself, constitute a sufficient reason to approve indigenous strategy. Experience indicates that indigenous methods usually lead to more rapid numerical growth, more genuine expansion growth, and a more culturally relevant growth. Local Christians assume responsibility. The church is their church—not a foreign copy. Church services are in cultural forms, natural and recognizable to them. Reproducibility is more easily attained because obstructions to outreach are minimized.

Indigenous strategies encourage natural witness by the entire body of Christians. Every believer is brought into the plan of witnessing. Leadership remains in local hands and witness more adapted to culture. Even church discipline is in local hands and more in line with local ways.

Indigenous strategy is correct strategy. It is proper because it is biblical. Roland Allen shows that Paul's methodology followed basically an indigenous plan.[23] Indigenous patterns violate no biblical or ethical principle. Therefore, since this strategy is biblically and ethically acceptable and since it seems to produce a more effective result, indigenous patterns should be considered when missionary strategy is planned.

Reaching Toward Indigenous Patterns

An indigenous church is an ideal toward which church growth reaches. McGavran correctly expresses the concern that the indigenous pattern might become a "new idol." He pleads that mission strategy guard against any position such as, "We will adhere to indigenous principles whether churches grow or not."[24]

Indigenous principles are sound. They are, however, only one factor in growth or nongrowth. Thus, McGavran concludes:

> Indigenous church principles are good, but it is a serious oversimplification to imagine that they are the only factor or even the chief factor in growth or nongrowth. The tremendous role played by revival should not be overlooked. Nor can the weaknesses of the "one-by-one against the social tide" mode of conversion in tightly organized societies be forgotten. Many other factors also affect growth.[25]

In the main, mission strategy is well advised to work toward an indigenous pattern. Realizing that perfect attainment to any pattern is seldom reached, the indigenous pattern should remain the goal. Any Church or Mission can reach toward an indigenous pattern by using whichever of the following suggestions apply to them.

Commit to the effort of change to indigenous patterns.—All change is difficult. Major change is traumatic. Change seldom takes place apart from commitment to that change. One hundred percent commitment to indigenous ideas should not be expected. Until a committed core determines that change is necessary, there is little chance for change toward indigenous patterns.

Deal compassionately, yet firmly, with old patterns.—Much of the mission work around the world has been based on some type of subsidy. The attempt to change, of necessity, involves interaction with these old patterns. There should be no criticism of those who promoted previous patterns nor pride in those advocating the new. The purpose is not to criticize or win. The purpose is to increase God's harvest.

Understanding and compassion toward all connected with the old should be sought. For some, any change will be undoing the pattern of years (even a lifetime) of service. For nationals, change may alter the entire method of ministry. Accept reluctance and even opposition to change as normal and understandable.

At the same time, be firm. To change in the direction of a more indigenous pattern is better for both the work and the workers. This conviction will provide courage to be determined to reach toward indigenous patterns.

Work openly, sympathetically, with national co-workers.—The change from Mission control to indigenous patterns should be a cooperative venture. Unilateral efforts seldom provide viable results. If the Mission forces indigenous patterns, resentment is likely and understandable. If the national convention seeks to appropriate power and authority, resistance likewise is probable. Patience on both sides will be necessary to change to new ways.

Expect the local churches to assume responsibility.—Missionaries should indicate their trust of the people. The goal of converting to indigenous patterns is responsibility by local people. This assumption should be encouraged. Converting to indigenous patterns is often delayed because of missionary fear that the work will not be tended. The problem is much like that of allowing a child to assume responsibilities. Trust begets responsibility.

Deal with subsidy and missionary life-style.—The crucial issue in converting to a more indigenous pattern usually relates to finances. Unilateral decisions here can result in damaged relationships. While opposition to new patterns should not be allowed to block change, consultation and understanding are imperative. In most cases, some form of phaseout on subsidy patterns is both necessary, considerate, and advisable.

The necessity to deal with missionary life-style along with subsidy is often overlooked. Reduction in subsidy usually burdens nationals. The issue can somewhat be alleviated if missionaries show their dedication by a reduction of their own life-styles. This reduction must not be insincere. It should, rather, be a deliberate act of identification. To cut subsidy and not missionary life-style shows a lack of feeling and comaraderie. I doubt that successful conversion to indigenous methods and reduction of subsidy can ever be accomplished without a comparable reduction of missionary life-style.

Accept and encourage cultural ways.—The process of indigenization should lead to new ways and hopefully more culturally appropriate ways. New patterns of worship, church government, pastor-congregation relations, meeting times, and other aspects may arise. Missionaries should not simply allow but rather should welcome change to more culturally appropriate patterns.

Efforts to rid a Christian movement of paternalism and Western ways pays dividends in increased evangelistic effectiveness. Missionaries must realize that their responsibility includes communicating the true message and providing a source of cultural alternatives for the people—if they need and want them. The missionary must be aware that an outsider can make no cultural decisions for the church. While the missionary may provide guidance and value judgments, he remains the advocate. The change, innovation, comes through the people themselves. It is imperative that missionaries accept and encourage the cultural patterns of an indigenous approach since this approach changes from the traditional colonial paternalism with which western missions have historically approached the task. Indigenous ways fit culture.

Expect some stress and adjustment.—Change from a mission-centered method to an indigenous pattern inevitably results in stress for both nationals and missionaries. In most cases, neither nationals nor missionaries can convert in one act. The movement toward the indigenous church requires a series of adjustments. The wise agents of change, missionaries and nationals, recognize the adjustment problems and try to structure the change process to allow some gradualism into the new pattern.

Trust the Holy Spirit in the entire process.—Missionary reluctance to accept the full implications of the indigenous pattern often is based on a lack of trust in the Holy Spirit. The Church (church) and people should be allowed to hear and follow the Spirit's lead. Faith in the leading of the Spirit and the ability of the Christians to hear and follow that leading is imperative to indigenization.

Conclusion

The indigenous pattern is more than a catchword for modern missions. Correctly understood and applied, the indigenous approach is a valid and important strategy. The approach, like other strategies, should not be deified, but rather used in accord with the needs of the church. Indigenous strategy provides a legitimate goal toward which most mission efforts should aim. Testing the indigenous strategy indicates it to be a valid method.

People Movement Strategy

At least two thirds of all converts to Christianity in Asia, Africa, and Oceania have come through what Church Growth writers call "people movements." People movement growth has likewise been significant in Latin America, Europe, Asia Minor, and North Africa.[26] McGavran is convinced that people movement strategy provides quality as well as numerical growth.[27] A strategy providing such significant growth of necessity demands study, testing, and, if it proves a valid strategy, implementation.

What Are People Movements

Misunderstanding of people movement theory resulted from the early use of the term, *mass movements.* J. Waskom Pickett entitled his seminal book, *Christian Mass Movements in India.* In 1956 Pickett and others produced a study entitled, *Church Growth and Group Conversion.* References to "group conversion" and "mass movements" will also be found in McGavran's, *The Bridges of God.* These books and these terms gave rise to questions concerning people movements especially in the individualized West. To some, the concept seemed to promote wholesale additions of masses of unconverted into churches. Western theologians experienced particular strain with the idea of people movements.

Because of confusion about the concept and in order to precisely express the idea, Church Growth Writers replaced the term *mass movement,* with *people movement.* People movement, while still employed, also does not accurately convey the meaning of the strategy. Thus was born the rather involved term, multi-individual, mutually interdependent conversion.

This term speaks of a conversion pattern of many individual decisions being expressed mutually. The contrast is a pattern of decision by a solitary individual, expressed often in the face of family or social disapproval. In the multi-individual decision pattern, each person comes to an individual choice and commitment. Salvation comes only through personal commitment to Christ.

Mutually interdependent means that the people expressing the commitment are intimately known to one another and take the step in view of what the others are doing. McGavran concludes:

> Mutually interdependent means that all those taking the decision are intimately known to each other and take the step in view of what the other is going

to do. This is not only natural; it is moral. Indeed, it is immoral, as a rule, to decide what one is going to do regardless of what others do.[28]

A people movement, then, is not a mass conversion nor a group conversion. Neither masses nor groups can be saved. A people movement is a joint expression of a series of multi-individual mutually interdependent conversions. This strategy speaks more to how decisions to become Christian are expressed than to the process of conversion itself. The joint expression opens the doors for a culturally acceptable and approved way to express commitment to Christ.

Examples of People Movements

Christian history provides innumerable examples of people movements. McGavran points to the early church as a people movement among Jewish people. Of the early, Jewish church McGavran states:

> The early Church grew *within* Judaism. For at least a decade the Jews who were becoming Christians were not conscious at all of joining a non-Jewish religion. Had they dreamed that this was a possibility many of them would never have become Christians. Even after they were changed by fellowship with the Living Christ, they refused to accept Gentile Christians as full members of the Jewish Christian people! The bearing of this on the growth of People Movements today is significant. It shows that peoples become Christian fastest when least change of race or clan is involved. When it is felt that "we are moving with our people and those who have not come now will come later," then the Church grows most vigorously.[29]

McGavran confirms that the enlargement of the Christian faith to include the Gentiles began in earnest with a people movement in Antioch, when "the fire first jumped across social lines."[30] The people movements that brought Cornelius and the Antioch Greeks into the Faith were unplanned. These movements do, however, follow the general pattern now recognized as people movements.

Another example of the people movement happened in Burma where Adoniram Judson went as a missionary to the cultured, Buddhist Burmese. Judson took little notice of the uneducated, animistic Karen people. Ko Tha Bya, a Karen who associated with Judson, spoke to the Karen people while Judson preached to the Burmese. Judson experienced few converts but many of the Karens accepted the message brought by Ko Tha Bya. Today, there is a mighty movement to Christ among the Karens and related tribes.

Hundreds of thousands have come into the churches and become fine Christians.[31]

In the Central Celebes (Indonesia) the Central Celebes Church (Geredja Kristen Sulawesi Tengah) grew out of a people movement pattern. The missionaries, Albert C. Krugt and H. Adriani, were convinced the Church should be based on indigenous patterns. They were convinced that the message and the approach should be purged of foreign elements. The missionaries recognized that the Torodja society was collective rather than individualistic. For this reason they believed the movement should follow family and clan lines. So deep was this conviction that they delayed baptism until an entire group was ready to follow together. After seventeen years, in 1909, 180 persons from one village were baptized. The movement began to grow until by 1970 the membership reached over 130,000 persons in above 350 congregations.[32] The people movement pattern is obvious.

People movements are not restricted to undeveloped peoples, although these societies are most open to the pattern. David Wilkerson's experiences with the street gangs show similarities to people movement patterns.

Applying People Movement Strategy

People movements are God-given. They cannot be planned or forced—only encouraged. No strategy will ensure their occurrence. Missionary strategy can, however, allow, expect, and accept such movements when they are granted by the Lord. People movement patterns lead to genuine growth through conversion and ethical change.

People movement patterns often develop among groups with strong extended family lines. McGavran speaks of "webb movements" in which the gospel moves across lines of relationship. Such relational groupings are apparent in many levels among many groups of people.[33]

In urban areas the key may be to find the groupings and work among them. Evangelizing the city street gang may await something of the nature of a people movement among them. Even in the so-called individualized West, multi-individual, mutually interdependent conversion patterns are possible and valuable in reaching the lost.

In applying people movement strategies, the following steps should be observed:

1. Accept the possibility and validity of men and women jointly expressing their faith in Christ. Realize that in many cultures one would not think of not checking with the group before a decision. Refuse to allow the

cultural overhang of Western individualism to cloud the realization of the validity of people movements. George Peters says, "There is an ethnic, a group, a people approach in evangelism which has been either overlooked or ignored by the Westerner, not because it is not in the Bible, but because of his mentality of individualism."[34]

2. Be aware of groupings, families, gangs, and other communities through which the gospel can spread. Such groups exist in nearly every society. They represent unusual possibilities for church growth.

3. Approach the recognized groups as social units. Work through the recognized leaders of the group. Adapt to the structure of their society. Speak to the individuals as members of the group.

4. Take a positive approach to communicating God's message. Attacking the existing beliefs, behaviors, and concepts most often proves fruitless. Present the message of a loving God, a saving Christ, and a leading Spirit.

5. Consider waiting on baptism until a sizable group can respond together. Care must be taken, however, that baptism not be understood as some kind of graduation. Allow time for the group to develop.

6. Provide continuing post-baptismal care. Teaching, shepherding, and guidance are imperative. McGavran declares that the quality of a people movement is uniquely tied to and dependent on post-baptismal care.[35] The post-baptismal care should be adapted to the needs of the people served.

Conclusion

Accepting the possibility of people movements is wise strategy. Such movements are important to the furtherance of the gospel. Continued research into the people movement pattern should be undertaken in order to discover additional applications in both more and less developed countries.

Discipling Then Perfecting Strategy

Church Growth Writers, such as McGavran, have tended to emphasize discipling (evangelizing) to be followed by perfecting (guiding to spiritual growth and development).[36] This strategy primarily relates to people coming to Christ and his church from other religions with meager understanding of the full message of Christianity. The important step is bringing them to a commitment to Jesus and his salvation. Detailed ethical and doctrinal teaching can be given during the perfecting stage. The strategy attempts to avoid the restrictive tendency to demand detailed knowledge of Christianity and advanced ethical attitudes and behaviors.

Some missionaries have placed excessive demands on new converts. They denied the people church membership or baptism until they put away second wives, stopped smoking, refrained from dancing, or evidenced some other ethical transformation.[37] Conversion leads to changed behavior. The gospel brings social and cultural transformation. These changes do not, however, always happen immediately. The discipling then perfecting strategy simply suggests that the entire body of teaching—both doctrinal and ethical need not be required before the person is accepted as a believer.

Furthermore, this strategy insists that attention be given to teaching and training converts in Christian doctrine and living. The real point of the discipling then perfecting strategy relates to accepting believers as believers on their own profession of faith, baptising them on their testimony to that faith, and then helping them to the fullest expression of that faith in life and thought.

Concern has been expressed as to the theological and ethical implications of the discipling then perfecting strategy. John H. Yoder expressed fear that this emphasis draws too drastic a line between salvation and sanctification. He correctly sees the two aspects of salvation as part of one total experience. Yoder further is concerned lest the delay in ethical instruction and demand lead to "cheap grace," whereby one might come into the faith without full understanding of its demands. The concern on Yoder's part is understandable for he seems to hear McGavran saying that the presentation of the gospel should accommodate persons who hold to southern racism or militant anticommunism in order to win them to commitment.[38]

Yoder's concerns are legitimate and proper. In essence, the discipling then perfecting strategy is not intended to manipulate people into church membership by disguising Christianity's full demands. The strategy, rather, seeks to allow people and groups to come to their own understanding of the demands of faith and in their own ways change lives and cultures to the biblical patterns. Church Growth does not divide the discipling and perfecting patterns as distinct acts but only sees that the second is based on the first and the first certainly not precluding the second.

Missionaries sometimes require of new converts deeper ethical change than is demonstrated by church members in the sending Churches. The problem is that often certain ethical and theological patterns are demanded and other equally important patterns overlooked. Missionaries, who themselves are critical, covetous, or ungenerous, may demand new converts stop some customary act in order to become a member of the church.

The discipling then perfecting strategy suggests that people be brought to faith and church membership. The perfecting stage then leads these people to more fully express the total dimensions of the Faith. While Yoder's concerns are well-taken, I think the strategy, correctly understood and implemented, is not only acceptable, but due extensive use.

Questions and Activities

1. Identify homogeneous groups in your area. Should these groups be approached in differing ways?
2. Describe a church that would be indigenous for a wealthy, American neighborhood.
3. Read James Sunda's *Church Growth in West New Guinea.* Note the way the people movement developed.
4. Respond to McGavran's statement that two thirds of all converts in Asia, Africa, and Oceania have come to Christ through people movements. If the statement is true, does that fact make these movements acceptable?

Further Reading

Alan R. Tippett, *Verdict Theology in Missionary Theory* (William Carey Library)
C. Peter Wagner, *Church Growth and the Whole Gospel* (Harper and Row)
James Sunda, *Church Growth in West New Guinea* (Lucknow Publishing House)
Don Robinson, *Peace Child* (Regal)
Melvin Hodges, *The Indigenous Church* (Gospel Publishing House)
Roland Allen, *Missionary Methods: St. Paul's or Ours* (Eerdmans Publishing House)

Notes

1. C. Peter Wagner, *Your Church Can Grow* (Glendale, Calif.: Regal Books, 1976), p. 110.
2. C. Peter Wagner, *Our Kind of People* (Atlanta: John Knox Press, 1979), pp. 39-50,110-13.
3. McGavran, *Understanding Church Growth,* pp. 59-75.

4. Ralph Elliott, *Church Growth That Counts* (Valley Forge: Judson Press, 1981), pp. 55-63.

5. Edward R. Dayton, "Planning Strategies for Evangelism," in *Unreached Peoples 80,* ed. C. Peter Wagner and Edward R. Dayton (Elgin, Ill.: David C. Cook Publishing Co., 1980), p. 25.

6. McGavran, *Understanding Church Growth,* p. 223.

7. Francis M. DuBose, *How Churches Grow in an Urban World* (Nashville: Broadman Press, 1978), p. 126.

8. McGavran, *Understanding Church Growth,* p. 7.

9. Larry L. McSwain, "A Critical Appraisal of the Church Growth Movement," *Review and Expositor* LXXVII, 4 (Fall 1980):521-37.

10. B. V. Subbamma, *New Patterns for Discipling Hindus* (South Pasadena, Calif.: William Carey Library, 1970), pp. xii, 33-37,52-78.

11. McGavran, *Understanding Church Growth,* pp. 242-43.

12. T. B. Maston, *Christianity in the Modern World* (New York: The Macmillan Co., 1957), pp. 144-45.

13. McGavran, *Understanding Church Growth,* pp. 234-35.

14. Ibid., pp. 235-36.

15. Ebbie C. Smith, *God's Miracles: Indonesian Church Growth,* pp. 84-94.

16. Paul Minear, *The Obedience of Faith* (London: SCM Press, 1971), p. 8.

17. C. Peter Wagner, *Our Kind of People,* p. 150.

18. William A. Smalley, "Cultural Implications of the Indigenous Church," *Practical Anthropology* 5, 2 (1958): 54.

19. Allan R. Tippett, *Verdict Theology in Missionary Theory,* pp. 154-58.

20. Ibid., p. 156.

21. C. Peter Wagner, *Frontiers of Missionary Strategy* (Chicago: Moody Press, 1971), pp. 163-64.

22. McGavran, *Understanding Church Growth,* pp. 378-82.

23. Roland Allen, *Missionary Methods: St. Paul's or Ours?* pp. 49-61.

24. McGavran, *Understanding Church Growth,* p. 383.

25. Ibid.

26. Ibid., p. 336.

27. Ibid., p. 334.

28. Ibid., p. 340.

29. Donald A. McGavran, *The Bridges of God* (New York: Friendship Press, 1955), pp. 22-23.

30. Ibid., p. 23.

31. McGavran, *Understanding Church Growth,* p. 397.

32. Smith, *God's Miracles: Indonesian Church Growth,* pp. 78-80.

33. McGavran, *Understanding Church Growth,* pp. 360-62.

34. George W. Peters, *Saturation Evangelism* (Grand Rapids: Zondervan Publishing House, 1970), pp. 173-74.

35. McGavran, *Understanding Church Growth,* pp. 364-66.

36. Ibid., p. 170.

37. Robert Redford, *The Village that Chose Progress* (Chicago: The University of Chicago Press, 1950), pp. 88-113.

38. John H. Yoder, "Church Growth Issues in Theological Perspective," in *The Challenge of Church Growth: A Symposium,* ed. Wilbert R. Shenk (Scottdale, Penn.: Herald Press, 1973), pp. 36-38.

4
Discovering the Whys of Church Growth

The growth (or decline) of any Church (or church) is reflected in the facts of growth. These facts, related to the growth of churches and denominations, often lie hidden, and thus unheeded, in records and memories. The imperative lessons contained in these facts about growth, therefore, regrettably remain locked away and unused. This chapter relates ways of discovering and using the facts of growth—the whys of church growth.[1]

Finding, facing, and evaluating the facts of growth is a spiritual undertaking. Few procedures are more wasteful than continuing year after year with no genuine effort to analyze methods, evaluate results, or seek more productive patterns. It is therefore necessary that every religious organization analyze what it is doing, how it is doing it, and ways the harvest might be increased. In fact, refusal to seek and act on the facts of growth is basically unfaithfulness to God.

The facts of growth should be investigated without any sense of criticism or fault-finding. The purpose of studying church growth is neither to praise nor to blame but only to understand. However, when it is evident that some method has not resulted in significant church growth, or that an adjustment in method would likely increase effectiveness, faithfulness to the Lord of the harvest demands that recommendations and actions to that end be forthcoming.

A willingness to evaluate honestly, analyze correctly, and adjust courageously is a prerequisite for progress and proper growth. Studying the facts of growth provide opportunity to understand the past in order to influence the future. As methods and their results are scrutinized, both strengths and weaknesses become apparent. Old methods can be corrected, new methods discovered.

Providing Background Material

Discovering the whys of church growth begins with a perceptive description of the church (or Church) and community related to the work of the group. The exact direction of the background study will be determined by the nature of the work being studied. Cross-cultural studies will contain more anthropological materials. The study of a church in the United States would involve more sociological insight.

In any case, the background material forms a foundation for the entire study as it relates how these historical, social, and cultural factors have affected and will affect the growth of the group. Valid plans for the future can only be formulated on the basis of accurate information and sound data concerning the culture, the setting, and basic understanding of the people.

Contents of Background Material

The background material focuses squarely on factors affecting the planting and developing of churches. It includes more than historical and ethnological materials. McGavran concludes:

> . . . The student of church growth is highly selective. He gathers only those facts which are needed to understand the thrusts of growth and recession. Instead of presenting a profusion of data, most of it irrelevant as concerns the increase of Christians, he presents only data having something to do with his theme.[2]

The background material should contain historical, sociological, anthropological, and religious information that relates to church growth. Church growth, while much more than a social or anthropological phenomenon, does take place within the differing societies of mankind. Therefore, to perceive why churches grow (or fail to grow), leaders must try to understand the historical situation, the social structure, and the cultural milieu of the peoples among whom the Church is laboring.

Background material includes a history of the region in which the group is working. This is not simply a history but a church growth history. It isolates those historical factors affecting the growth of churches. Thomas Bennett's *Tinder in Tabasco* relates how the persecution of Christians in Tabasco between 1924 and 1935 resulted in increased church growth.[3] Political events surrounding the Communist failure in Indonesia in 1965 stimulated growth in the churches of East Java.[4]

A detailed history of the group under study also provides needed insight.

The various regions opened, the institutions established, and the general pattern of the growth should be carefully noted. While this historical section will not attempt any detailed interpretation of the facts, it should present the group's history as a basis for later interpretation. Even unpleasant facts, such as splits, failures, and reverses should be noted.

The social structure of the peoples served must be clarified and related to church growth. Social structure relates to the power structure, marriage customs, kinship lines, land rights, and many other cultural factors that influence church growth. The people of Madura in Indonesia have remained solidly Islamic and furiously resistant to Christianity due at least partially to the strong extended family units that make up Madurese social structure. These strong extended family units exert extreme pressure on members to remain in the accepted religious pattern, that is, Islam. Christianity grows slowly in regions where to become a believer separates one from his/her people.[5]

Background material relates the historical, religious, and cultural factors to church growth. Finding ways to allow men to consider the gospel is one of the purposes of background material. McGavran contends that the great obstacles to conversion are social rather than theological. He believes great turning of Moslems and Hindus can be expected when ways are found for them to become Christian without renouncing their brethren, which seems to them a betrayal.[6] To find and suggest ways to allow men freedom to choose is the purpose of the background study in a survey.

The background material includes information on the community in which the church is located. This study is particularly important for an American church. Much of the community information can be obtained from city government, census materials, and city planning offices. Facts related to population figures, population movement, and population projections should be noted. Ethnic divisions, socio-economic factors, age, housing, and occupation factors likewise are important. This demographic material must be a vital part of any study of church growth.

Sources of Background Material

The needed background information lies tucked away in records, writings, and memories and only needs to be discovered for use. The history of the church, denomination, or Mission is often recorded in various writings. While these writings may not be written from a view of church growth, they will contain much important information and contribute to genuine understanding. The church growth researcher may have to allow for the particular biases and views of those who have written the histories.

Other facts about the history of the church reside in the memories of persons who were there during the years of growth (or decline). Again, the memories may be biased, but by asking the proper questions, one can uncover vast resources for understanding the past.

Sociological and anthropological materials provide vital understanding of the people and communities to be served. These facts and trends can be helpful, but should not be determinative in planning work. Remember, receptivity of people to the gospel is more important than mere numbers. Demographic facts discovered from census and other data can provide guidance and understanding.

Behavioral science studies help in understanding the nature of the society. Church growth studies must recognize the diverse groupings of people, their social structure, and other factors that relate to how they will react to the gospel. Sociological and anthropological studies must be part of the background picture of every church growth study.

Getting the Facts of Growth

Gathering the facts of growth is among the more demanding and yet most important phases of the effort to discover the whys of growth. Many of these facts are numerical. An objective, accurate, numerical approach is indispensable for understanding church growth. To any who scorn the statistical approach, McGavran answers:

> To be sure, no one was ever saved by statistics; but then, no one was ever cured by the thermometer to which the physician pays such close attention. X-ray pictures never knit a single broken bone, yet they are of considerable value to physicians in telling them how to put the two ends of a fractured bone together. Similarly, the facts of growth will not in themselves lead anyone to Christ. But they can be of marked value to any Church which desires to know where, when, and how to carry on its work so that maximum increase of soundly Christian churches will result.[7]

The Needed Facts

Understanding the whys of growth demands a multitude of facts. Before setting forth techniques for gathering these facts, it is necessary to isolate the needed facts.

The first body of facts relates to membership total figures. Virgil Gerber emphasized the importance of membership statistics, calling them "the bedrock of data" necessary for diagnosing the health of a church.[8] Membership figures are needed for at least eleven years—even longer for older Churches. To understand church growth, one must have membership totals for: (1) the entire Church; (2) each geographical, cultural or administrative area; (3) each local congregation; (4) each homogeneous unit.

While membership totals should include figures for each year, this is often impossible. When some figures are unavailable, statistics are gathered for as many years as possible. Figures at times seem to reveal discrepancies, but given time, the statistics will adjust themselves. Any year, or number of years, may be inaccurate; the general trend will be firm. Later entries correct earlier mistakes.

The second body of facts needed relates to information about new members. Statistics on the number of baptisms for as many years as possible are highly significant. Baptismal figures, however, must be redefined. This redefinition consists of drawing a distinction between biological growth and conversion growth. A Church truly grows only by baptisms from the world. The number of new members gained by transfer, called transfer growth, must also be clarified.

A third body of facts needed relates to other aspects of Church development. The stability of the Church's membership must be considered. Statistics on the number of members who leave the membership of the Church and how and why they leave are vital information. Facts about members who transferred to other Churches, who reverted to the world, or who died, must be compiled. These statistics, often among the most difficult to find, add significantly to the understanding of church growth.

A Church (or church) might consider itself to be growing rapidly because of large numbers entering by baptism. However, if research indicates almost equal numbers reverting to the world, the authenticity of growth would be questioned. Thus, information on membership stability is necessary.

Factual information on the faithfulness of members is needed. The number of members who actually attend the services of the churches and who take part in church activities reveals much. Some indication of the spiritual growth of Christians is instructive. The evangelistic activity and fruitfulness of members should be measured and recorded.

A great deal about Church growth is learned from information concerning number of congregations and workers, especially those sometimes called "lay workers." The church should compare the number of workers and the worker-hours used to support the church's life and its own members with the number of workers and worker-hours directed to the lost. Figures showing the number of congregations and workers, year by year, indicate the growth pattern. Statistics relating to the level of giving by the members must be ascertained and reported.

The study should include some information as to how the churches are developing in regard to teaching, training, and social ministries. The number of members involved in systematic Bible study compared with total membership figures aids in understanding church development. The ability of the congregations to carry out the usual responsibilities of churches should be sought and reported.

The fourth body of facts needed relates to the families of the members. Family analysis lends important insights into church growth. The degree to which members are interrelated reveals the lines along which the gospel is spreading and churches are growing. Information regarding the number of full families in the membership and the number of split homes in which a part of the family belongs to the church is also significant.

The fifth body of facts needed relates to the Church organization and the mission organizations. It is important to know for what purposes the personnel and funds of each organization are being used. Facts about plans and procedures of each organization must be known and described. If more than one organization exists, there must be an understanding of projects and areas in which each is working independently and in which they are cooperating. In foreign mission work, the total working arrangement of the national organization and the mission organization must be clarified.

The sixth body of facts needed relates to church workers. Statistics about the percentage of national and missionary workers indicate whether leadership is more national or missionary oriented. The numbers of ordained and unordained workers must be discovered. The increase or decrease in workers is important. Levels of education, schools attended, age, years of experience in the ministry, and years served at the present position reveal important facts about development. The primary type of ministry of each missionary or staff worker should be clarified.

A seventh body of facts relates to the comparison of the growth to the general population. A failure to keep up percentage-wise with the types of people and institutions helps determine the strategies and ministries needed. Church growth thinking must take into account the nature of the populations to be served.

Financial records are the eighth body of facts of growth. Increased giving usually indicates increased participation and commitment. Equally instructive are facts of how the money actually is used. If monies are used primarily on facilities or other "self-serving" matters rather than service projects, the spirit of the group can be perceived. Financial records tell much about an organization.

The foregoing represents a mountain of factual material. At first glance, one might be tempted to despair. Actually, the task of gathering these facts, while formidable, is not impossible.

Sources of the Facts of Growth

The facts of growth are available, if not always readily available. Seeking and finding the facts of growth is an exhausting and demanding task. The rewards of this revealing undertaking make it more than worth the effort.

Statistical and historical records assist in finding the facts of growth. Records of membership totals, baptisms, numbers of congregations, workers, giving, assignment of personnel, and numerous other facts lie hidden and ready to be uncovered in Church and mission records. Denominational reports usually include statistical summaries. Local churches often have yearly reports that reveal growth facts.

The facts relating to church growth can also be discovered through the use of questionnaires and interviews. These techniques provide definite information, not only about membership figures, but also concerning facts and opinions of members. The manuals by Chaney and Lewis, Wagmire and Wagner, and Allen and Bullard provide suggestions for questionnaires for members, leaders, and others who can give pertinent facts about growth.

Conclusion

Getting the facts of growth is obviously not an easy matter. Through the use of historical and statistical records, and sociological research techniques, the survey proceeds to objectify them so that they can be more effectively studied and interpreted.

Visualizing the Facts of Growth

The importance of visualizing the facts of growth clearly, accurately, and strikingly cannot be overemphasized. Interpretation and evaluation are sharpened when the facts stand out in simple, understandable forms. Among several techniques for visualizing the facts of growth are simple graphs of growth, average annual growth rate, graphs of rates of growth (semi-logarithmic graphs), percentages, ratios, distributions, and comparative analyses of growth.

Simple Graphs of Growth

Church growth research relies heavily on graphs of growth which show membership facts over a period of time. No other technique clarifies and pictures growth facts so productively. Regarding the value of graphs, McGavran says:

> Columns of figures giving the membership of any church and its homogeneous units contain locked-up knowledge. By careful study the figures can be forced to reveal their secrets, but the process is tedious. When, however, each set of figures is transformed into a graph of growth, the secrets leap out at the reader. He who would understand church growth should construct line graphs showing at a glance what has transpired. He can then ask why it happened.[9]

Church growth studies can effectively use all types of graphs, line, bar, pie, etc.

The process of constructing graphs is relatively simple. Using graph paper (or other carefully divided surface), construct a horizontal scale representing the years of the church's (or denomination's) existence. Construct a vertical scale on which the number of members is plotted. Indicate the membership by placing a dot on the graph according to each year's membership and joining the dots. A visual of the church's growth appears in the line or bar graph produced. Vergil Gerber's book, *God's Way to Keep a Church Going and Growing,* provides simple, easily understood guidance in the construction and use of graphs. The manuals mentioned previously also provide help in graphing.

Line and bar graphs can picture information such as baptisms, giving, attendance, enrollment, etc. More than one type of information can be recorded on the same graph, such as Sunday School enrollment, church membership, and baptisms. One must be careful, however, not to include so much material on any one graph as to be confusing. Line graphs clearly show each rise, decline and plateau in growth. Such trends must be seen before understanding and planning can be effective. The pictures formed by line graphs provide the starting point for church growth thinking. Graphs objectify the facts as well as any other method. Church growth studies must make full use of these tools. As McGavran has said, "All thinking about the church should be done against the graph of growth, because when done without exact knowledge of how the church has and has not grown, it is likely to find itself in error."[10]

Line and bar graphs do not exhaust the possibilities for objectifying the facts of growth. Pie graphs are useful in depicting percentages. Graphs comparing the situation in various regions sometimes produce striking revelations. In Roy Shearer's study of church growth in Korea, the graphs comparing the regions of the nation showed that the phenomenal growth in the Korean church during the period had taken place primarily in the three northern provinces.[11] This type of information is vital.

A graph of membership flow gives helpful insight into the growth of a church. Membership flow graphs depict the additions and losses in membership together with notation of the kind of growth and loss. A typical membership flow graph would look as appears below.

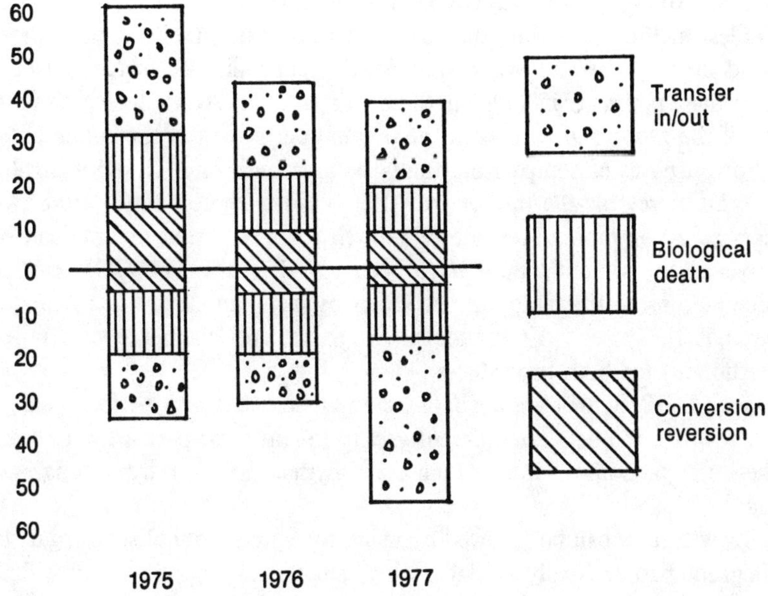

Growth Rates

Growth rates help significantly in the process of depicting the growth process. Obviously, the church of 100 that adds 50 members in a one-year period has a faster growth rate than one of 1,000 that adds 50 members in the same period. Thus, accurate growth rates contribute to accurate thinking about church growth.

The annual growth rate (AGR) of a denomination or a congregation is significant both for the group itself and for comparison with others. This figure is computed by subtracting the first year's membership (or that from any other time period) from the second year's and dividing the increase by the earlier figure. The decimal obtained can be converted to a percentage by multiplying by 100. A bar graph, showing the AGR for each of a number of years, can be instructive.

Another valuable calculation is the average annual growth rate (AAGR), which shows how many people per year come into the group's membership. The AAGR figures the percentage of growth related to membership. The simplest method of finding the AAGR uses prepared tables such as those found in Wagmire and Wagner or Smith (Appendix A). Instructions for using these tables are included in the manuals. The AAGR allows comparison of the group's growth with the population growth of the community.

For purposes of comparison, the decadal growth rate (DGR) is invaluable. DGR reveals the rate of growth across a period of time—from two years to 20 or more. The rate of growth for any period of time can be converted to what it would have been for 10 years. The DGR can be calculated using the table for AAGR or by using an electronic calculator that has the y^x and Y^x functions. Wagmire and Wagner give detailed instructions for both procedures.[12]

Once DGR figures are available, comparisons between periods of time can be made and between different groups for the same period can be seen. These comparisons tell much about the growth of the Church and congregations.

Growth rates can be pictured by using the special tool of semi-logarithmic graph paper, usually available where engineering supplies are provided. When growth facts are plotted on semi-logarithmic graph paper, the picture shows rate of growth rather than simply record of growth. While a line graph shows continual increase, the semi-logarithmic graph reflects a slowing or increasing rate of growth. Such information significantly relates to growth studies.

Rates of growth also help in understanding the growth process. Simply knowing the numbers of increase or decline sometimes clouds rather than reveals. A denomination must look not only at the amount of increase but at the rate of growth the increase reflects.

Percentages, Ratios, Frequencies

Percentages reveal the significance of much factual material. When a group realizes that 50 percent or more of new members drop out of the fellowship within a year, a new strategy is indicated. The congregation that learns that 85 percent of the members had no soul-winning experience in an entire year might be shocked into activity.

A note of caution, however: The way percentages are presented alters meaning. Both statements, "Fifteen percent of the membership is a result of transfer growth" and "Eighty-five percent of the members have never been members of any other church" relate to the same data. These statements, however, produce vastly different interpretations. Ratio statements also reveal significant aspects of church growth data. For example, the ratio of resident and nonresident members points out the health of a church. The ratio between resident members and baptisms likewise holds significance. Comparison of members to population and congregations to population can show a group something of its growth pattern. Further, the ratio of members to trained leaders and leaders who work inside the church membership to members engaged in outreach indicates strength or weakness.

Distribution figures can help a church determine such information as the age groupings of members. A bar graph showing the number of members in each age grouping may reveal certain age groups who are not being reached. A study of percentages, ratios, and distributions helps in understanding the growth of any group.

Interpreting the Facts of Growth

Survey effort, up to this point, actually constitutes an all-important preliminary. The facts, carefully gathered and clearly depicted, must now be analyzed as to their meaning and evaluated with regard to planning and goal setting. Interpreting the facts of growth occupies a central place in a Church Growth study.

Analyzing

Graphs, ratios, percentages, distributions tell when and by how much Churches and congregations have grown or declined. These helps do not tell "why" and "why" constitutes the primary and critical question. Thus, the first step in interpreting the facts of growth is analyzing the meaning of these facts.

Using the data that has been made visible, one studying church growth seeks answers or reasons for the revealed results. No one cause is generally sufficient to explain why a group grew or failed to grow in a given locality and time. Church growth is, as McGavran has stated, a "complex faithfulness."[13] Every increase, plateau, and decline should be closely investigated to find the reasons for the facts. Every aspect of growth should be considered.

The analysis phase of the study seeks understanding in order to stimulate growth. The study seeks to understand periods of stagnation and decline so as to avoid similar times in the future. It considers the periods of growth to find ways to increase the harvest.

Analysis must avoid the tendency to defend any theory of mission work as it avoids any defense of existing patterns. The analysis, to be effective, must be objective. People are important and feelings are a part of people. Still, the growth of Christ's church is the all-important factor, and nothing must be allowed to stand in the way of the analysis that can lead to greater evangelistic results.

The analysis process uses all the information on the Church, the local congregation, the various regions, the different homogeneous groups, to seek explanations for each rise, period of stagnation, and decline. The goal of the analysis is to find out the "why." Invalid reasons are set aside. Care must be taken to guard against simplistic reasoning. Clusters of reasons impacting growth or non-growth must be sought. The task of analysis is demanding; it is, however, the all-important step if church growth is to be considered.

As the student of church growth seeks to explain the spurts and the plateaus in church growth, a useful tool for comparing growth rates and explaining advance or decline is found in *Understanding Church Growth and Decline* by Dean R. Hoge and David A. Roozen.[14] Four factors that can influence growth are delineated: national contextual factors, national institutional factors, local contextual factors, and local institutional factors.

National contextual factors are events, situations, and happenings on the national level that affect church growth. Wars, changing birth rates, migration, recessions, and such affect church growth, but there is little the church can do about the situation.

National institutional factors include denomination-wide characteristics such as polity, theological orientation, controversies, standards, and mission emphases. Such matters affect church growth, but again, the local congregation can often do little to eliminate or alieviate the situation.

Local contextual factors significantly relate to church growth. Local community make-up and change, economic factors that influence the local community, plant closings and openings, and other such matters can either inhibit or stimulate church growth. Again, the congregation may find it can do little about these situations.

Local institutional factors relate to the congregation—its spirit, methods, dedication, and commitment to the Lord's work. When a congregation finds that something in its life or method is slowing growth, the congregation can and must do something to change the situation. Local institutional factors must never be allowed to inhibit church growth.

Obviously, in analyzing church growth, local institutional factors stand out. These factors must be thoroughly tested and honestly faced. Changes must be inacted when something in the life and work of the church stands in the way of growth.

Methods of analysis can be illustrated by studying the graph of the Protestant Church on Nias, an island off the northwest coast of Sumatra (mentioned in chapter 1). The Nias graph shows very slow growth from the beginning there of Christianity in 1871 until 1915. The sudden surge of growth in 1915 slowed to a plateau between 1920 and 1925. After 1925 the graph reveals continued growth until the present.

Several factors explain the growth of the Nias Church. The slow beginning can be attributed to the state of the island before the Dutch established control. The missionaries were unable to serve outside the coastal cities. Many Niasans were headhunters. After the Dutch established law and built roads, the mission work proceeded until 1915, when some 5,000 members were counted.

In 1915 a great revival, known as "The Great Repentance," broke out. Under the influence of this revival, the membership of the Church leaped to 62,000 by 1921. (This was an average annual growth rate of 52 percent). However, in 1925, the Church reported only 65,000 members. Such a

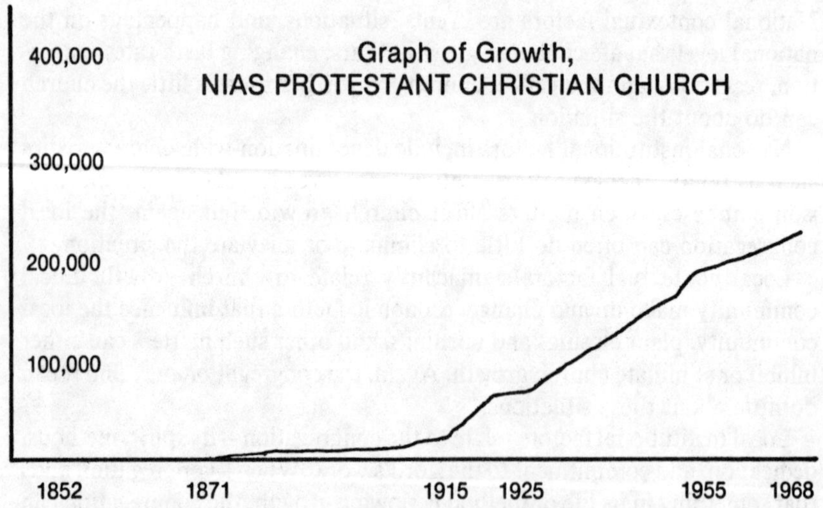

plateau would ordinarily be attributed to a decline in growth rate. The records revealed no tendency toward consolidation. Neither did records reveal any doctrinal, relational, or other problems. There seemed to be no explanation for this striking plateau in the growth of the Nias Church. However, secular history recorded an extended epidemic of flu that hit the island around 1919 and raged until 1923. Thousands died. This most likely explains the plateau. Although growth continued, death was removing unusually large numbers from the membership. After 1925, the epidemic eased and membership increase resumed. The Church was growing during the entire period of the epidemic, but membership figures remained static due to unusually heavy death rates.[15] This is the record of tremendous growth. Even so, from 1925 to 1968, the growth from 65,000 to 260,000 represents an average annual growth rate of only 3.3 percent.

The following graph of the growth of Baptist churches in two Indonesian cities (Semarang and Kediri) indicates spurts of growth around 1961 with a slowing between 1963-65, followed by a period of explosive growth.

Multiple factors must be considered in seeking reasons for this growth. In both cities, new evangelistic programs that emphasized planting churches began around 1961. The declining growth rate between 1963-65 can be partially explained by the slowing of these two programs due to the depar-

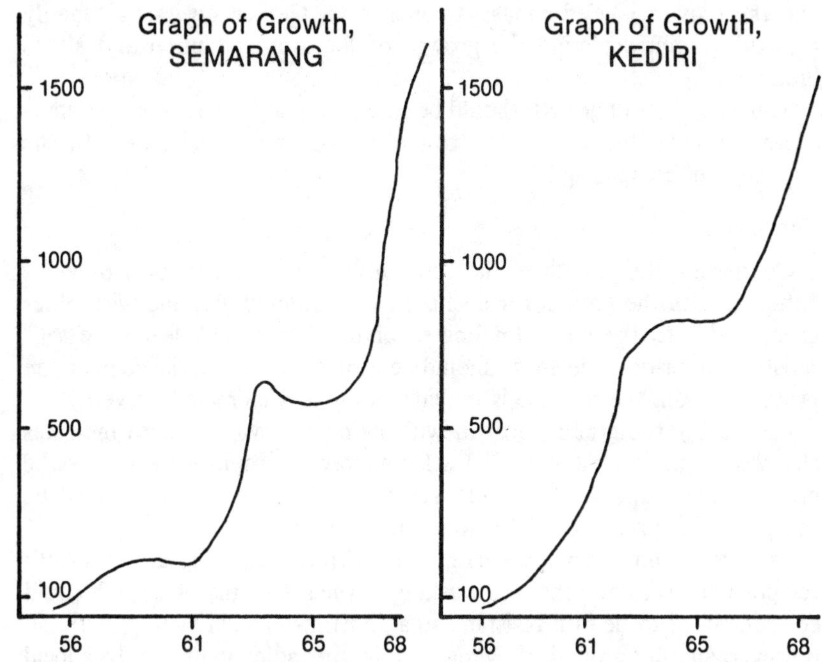

ture of leadership. Even more serious was the buildup of Communist pressure, leading to the attempted coup of September 1965. During the period of 1963-65, most churches in Indonesia reported a marked decline in growth.

The explosive growth following 1965 can be attributed to the increased responsiveness in many regions of Indonesia after the Communist failure. At the same time, a fruitful evangelistic campaign, emphasizing both personal evangelism and church planting, was promoted by the Baptist churches in 1966-67. This analysis of the growth of Baptist churches in two areas seeks beneath the surface for causes of growth and nongrowth.[16]

The full range of factors must be considered in seeking the reasons for growth, plateau, or decline. Analysis must consider every aspect of growth. Virgil Gerber points out that if the growth pattern of a church consists of rises and declines, one might conclude that the church was not growing healthily. However, if analysis indicates that periodically members go out of this church to start new congregations, the conclusion would be reversed and the growth labeled robust. In such case, Gerber suggests a "family growth" graph, depicting the growth of the mother church and all its branches.[17]

Thus, the facts of growth should be carefully analyzed in order to understand the whole picture. The process of analyzing is aided greatly by the technique of comparing.

Comparing

Comparing the growth of the Church (church) with its own previous patterns, with the growth (or decline) of the community, and with other groups adds to the understanding of church growth. A feeling of self-satisfaction, pride, or jealousy should be firmly set aside in the comparison process. Again, the purpose is understanding and increased harvest.

Comparing the group's growth with its own previous record indicates changes in growth rates. Declines from previous rapid growth must be noted, explained, and, if possible, reversed. More rapid growth must be accepted with praise to God who grants all growth.

The group should compare its growth with that of other groups—both religious and secular—that are working in the same area. A church could consider itself to be in a resistant area and thus explain slow growth. If, however, another group is growing rapidly, the indication might be a local institutional factor. In such a case, the church would want to adjust methods and/or seek revival in order to attain the growth desired by the Lord of the harvest. In this comparison with others, the object is to learn and improve.

The growth of the Church (church) should be compared to the growth of the population served. When population declines, church growth will often decline. A most serious situation exists when church growth declines in the face of population growth. A denomination should compare its growth to population—not only in terms of number of members, but also the ratio of congregations and population. The church that finds it has more persons in the community per church at present than was the case the year previously has reason for concern. Comparison thus leads to insight into growth.

Sharing

Interpreting the facts of growth extends to sharing the results of the study with members of the group, their supporting bodies, and all who are concerned about the growth of Christ's Church. A report should be written and distributed. This report will include the history, factual material, graphs, statistics, comparisons and analyses. Should there be different explanations for the growth patterns, these will be included. This report should be shared as widely as possible, especially by the group under study.

Acting on the Facts of Growth

The church growth study that stops with analyzing and sharing accomplishes little. The purpose of the study is more than another book or paper on church growth. The purpose of the study is action; the goal is change; the rationale is increase in the harvest.

Church growth studies, therefore, are designed to find and interpret the facts of church growth. They provide a foundation for decisions that lead to more effective methods for evangelism. Thus, when the survey reaches the point of decision making, it attains the purpose for which it was created.

These decisions include new goals, policies, and methods. Efforts of gathering, depicting, analyzing, and interpreting the facts of growth look toward this all-important step. To understand the facts of growth and to see ways of enlarging the harvest, and then to fail to make the decisions that will result in this greater harvest is to refuse to take the most vital and fruitful step.

Recommending

The study report usually should include recommendations to the Church, church, or mission. These recommendations should be stated in the form of objectives so as to make possible measurement of attainment. Recommendations should focus on changes that would help the Church grow bigger, better, and broader.

Recommendations should be positive, calling for doing something. They should be realistic yet challenging. There should be spiritual as well as numerical goals in the recommendations. The recommendations should be based squarely on the facts revealed by the survey. The group is encouraged to add other recommendations as they consider the report.

When the decisions have been made and written into policy statements and the goals, policies, and methods have been set, the survey, in one sense, is over. The most important function, however, awaits fulfillment—implementing the decisions. The next section considers ways and means of implementation.

Adopting

The recommendations growing out of the church growth study should be thoroughly discussed, perhaps modified, and finally adopted by the group. Thus, the denomination, congregation, or mission as a whole accepts the challenge and dedicates itself to attaining the goals.

There is little hope for change and increased harvest until the group (Church, church, mission) actually accepts the recommendations and sets goals for reaching them. The decision should be accepted as a spiritual commitment.

Implementing

Reaching the goals constitutes the single most important phase of the study. Failure to attain the goals and to implement the decisions means that the study has failed in its ultimate objectives. This is not to say that the study has been a total failure. The spiritual victories achieved, the insights acquired, the facts uncovered, and the unity gained, are all values in themselves. The ultimate objective, however, has not been attained until the study results in increased church growth.

Plans should be set for carrying out the goals projected by the study. Implementation is imperative.

Conclusion

Church growth studies involve extensive expenditures of time, effort, and material resources. Some might conclude that the mass of material demanded renders a study so involved as to be impractical or impossible. Such is not the case.

Any group can conclude an effective church growth study. Situations will sometimes make finding some facts or achieving some steps impossible. Such deletions decrease the overall effectiveness of the survey but do not obviate its ultimate value. Effective surveys can be realized although some steps are impossible and some facts unavailable.

The difficulties of carrying out a study should not deter a group from its effort. He who sees only the difficulties may turn back. The writer of Ecclesiastes notes: If you wait until the wind and the weather are just right, you will never plant anything and never harvest anything (11:4, GNB).

Every group should proceed with a church growth study. Church growth studies are possible, practical, and imperative. They open new avenues for attaining the will of God in evangelism and church development. The Holy Spirit works with power through efforts at self-study. For these and many other reasons, every group should engage in a church growth study.

Questions and Activities

1. Read a study of church growth. Several are mentioned in the "Further Reading" section. Note how the church growth facts were interpreted. What recommendations did you see?
2. Use one of the manuals (Waymire and Wagner, Chaney and Lewis, or Allen and Bullard) to make a study of your church.
3. Obtain census data on the area where your church is located. List the types of people the census indicates live in your area.
4. Why should a group make a church growth survey?

Further Reading

Bennett, Thomas. *Tinder in Tabasco* (Eerdmans)
Shearer, Roy E. *Wildfire: The Growth of the Church in Korea* (Eerdmans)
Gerber, Virgil. *God's Way to Keep a Church Growing and Going* (William Carey Library)
Hoge, Dean R. and Roozen, David A. *Understanding Church Growth and Decline: 1950-1978* (The Pilgrim Press)
Yeakley, Flavil R. *Why Churches Grow* (Christian Communications, Inc.)

Notes

1. Several manuals which provide detailed guidance in discovering and using the facts of growth are available. Ebbie C. Smith, *A Manual for Church Growth Survey* (William Carey Library, 1976) provides both the reasons for and the methods of conducting church growth surveys. Bob Waymire and C. Peter Wagner, *The Church Growth Survey Handbook* (The Global Church Growth Bulletin, Box 66, Santa Clara, CA 95982, 1980) provide step-by-step guidance on conducting studies with tables and graph paper for use. This manual is especially helpful in figuring growth rates. Charles L. Chaney and Ron S. Lewis have prepared *Manual for Design for Church Growth* (Broadman, 1977), which also provides detailed directions for church growth studies and is of particular help in community study. Jere Allen and George Bullard, *Shaping a Future for the Church in the Changing Community*

(Home Mission Board, Southern Baptist Convention) which guides in all phases of survey study is invaluable for any church—not only for transitional congregations.

2. Donald A. McGavran, *Understanding Church Growth,* pp. 109-110.

3. Thomas Bennett, *Tinder in Tabasco* (Grand Rapids: Wm. B. Eerdman's Publishing co., 1968.)

4. Frank L. Cooley, *Indonesia: Church and Society* (New York: Friendship Press, 1968), pp. 70, 90. See also Avery Willis, *Indonesian Revival: Why Two Million Came to Christ* (South Pasadena, Calif.: William Carey Library, 1977), p. 12.

5. Ebbie C. Smith, *God's Miracles: Indonesian Church Growth* (South Pasadena, Calif.: William Carey Library, 1970), pp. 12,110-11.

6. McGavran, *Understanding Church Growth,* pp. 223-44.

7. Ibid., p. 94.

8. Vergil Gerber, *God's Way to Keep a Church Going and Growing* (Glendale, Calif.: Regal Books, 1973), p. 43.

9. McGavran, *Understanding Church Growth,* p. 128.

10. Ibid., p. 130.

11. Roy Shearer, *Wildfire: The Growth of the Church in Korea* (Grand Rapids: Wm. B. Eerdman's Publishing Co., 1966), p. 136.

12. Waymire and Wagner, pp. 16-17.

13. McGavran, *Understanding Church Growth,* pp. 3-22.

14. Hoge and Roozen, "Some Sociological Conclusions about Church Trends," in *Understanding Church Growth and Decline: 1950-1978,* ed. Hoge and Roozen, pp. 324-27.

15. Smith, pp. 94-96.

16. Ibid., pp. 166-75.

17. Gerber, pp. 50-51.

5
Applying Behavioral Science Insights

Evangelism and church growth remain totally spiritual undertakings. These spiritual undertakings, however, happen within the "multitudinous societies of mankind."[1] Mankind lives in societies. People are connected to one another by ties of culture and social structure. Every attempt to evangelize and congregationalize must take culture and social structure into account.

The behavioral sciences assist missionaries and church leaders in attaining understanding of culture and societies so that they can most effectively communicate the gospel and develop churches in the diverse groupings of mankind. Behavioral science insights, while in no sense a substitute for the power of the Holy Spirit, are valid, needed, and constructive for Christian leaders. Therefore, church growth thinking recognizes the need of accurate knowledge about the people to be served—their culture, customs, situation, place of residence, worldview, and religious persuasions.

What Is Behavioral Science?

The term *behavioral science* describes several disciplines (sociology, psychology, anthropology) that study mankind, especially mankind in relationship or community. These disciplines provide insights into mankind—the inner workings of persons and the workings of persons with others. Of these, sociology and anthropology, which center mainly on man-in-community, especially provide helpful and significant insights for church growth.

Behavioral Science and Missions

It is proper that evangelism in cross-cultural settings make full use of insights provided by the behavioral sciences. While the Bible is the final authority, Win Arn and Donald A. McGavran point out that the marvelous explosion of knowledge in our day has come about in accordance with God's will and guidance. These writers contend that God expects us to use and apply the knowledge from various fields "in line with biblical principles." They conclude:

> When we use this knowledge—geography, anthropology, sociology, psychology, and many other areas—in line with biblical principles, we are doubly right. We are using the tools God has given us, and we are using them for ends that he blesses.[2]

Eugene Nida insists that good missionaries have always been good anthropologists. By this statement he means that effective missionaries have not only been aware of human needs but have also recognized the different approaches to meeting life's needs in different cultures. Furthermore, the more effective missionaries have immersed themselves both in a knowledge of the cultures they serve and in a meaningful relationship with the people and the culture.[3]

Concerning the missionary's need to use the insights of sociology and anthropology, the Roman Catholic missionary anthropologist Louis J. Luzbetak writes:

> Even centuries before the Science of Culture was born, the most effective missionaries were those blessed with a deep appreciation of the diversity of cultures and of the important role which cultures play in human behavior. The most successful apostolic approaches have always been the ones geared most closely to the character and needs of the particular life-way. Missionary effectiveness has always gone hand in hand with immersion in local culture. St. Paul, Ricci, de Nobili, and other great apostles of the past had, of course, no choice but to rely on their own *innate* anthropological sense; today, however, to rely on anything less than a *Science* of Culture would be as foolish as to rely on anything less than a *Science* of Medicine. . . . Cultural Anthropology is indeed a "missionary science" par excellence. There is no other art or science that can help the missioner divest himself of his cultural prejudices more surely than this science. Moreover, the cultural context (the subject-matter of this science) is one of the most basic tools of the missionary. No matter what his particular task may be, he is a professional "builder of a better world," and like all builders he too must constantly have recourse to his basic tools—his plumbline and his level—lest the building which he is constructing get out of line, or even collapse. The missioner's plumbline is Truth (theology, philosophy, science, prudence, and the aims of the apostolate); his level is the local cultural context.[4]

Such convictions as expressed above led Allan R. Tippett to declare anthropology as a "necessity," not a "luxury" for church missions.[5]

The behavioral sciences are not cure-alls for missionary strategy. No amount of scientific methodology can take the place of the Holy Spirit. Furthermore, the Holy Spirit can grant results in spite of our inadequate methods. Even the best of strategy (or methods) does not assure nor can it force a spiritual harvest. Cultural anthropology is certainly not the full answer to problems facing Christian missions. It can, however, significantly aid in the communication of the gospel to the people in various cultures of the world.

The behavioral sciences can and should contribute to missionary strategy both in the United States and in other countries as everyone engaged in cross-cultural ministries needs these insights. Behavioral sciences contribute to Christian missions in four basic ways.

Providing Cultural Understanding

The person seeking to minister effectively to a given people must gain an understanding of and identification with that people and their culture. A missionary without cultural understanding resembles the teacher without access to educational methods. Behavioral sciences can help provide this necessary cultural understanding.

Recognizing and Accepting Culture

Cultural understanding first aids missionaries to recognize and accept cultural differentiation. Culture has been called the learned and shared part of mankind's environment. Culture thus includes attitudes, values, ways of behaving, and methods of getting the job done. In summary, culture is that complex and integrated body of guides that includes knowledge, belief, art, morals, custom, language, and other capabilities acquired by persons as members of a society.

Mankind is distinctively a cultural being—that is to say that all groups of people have culture and culture is one of the major factors separating mankind from the rest of creation. Any cluster of people will have a set of rules that guide every aspect of their common life. As Peter Wagner has said, "From major life decisions, such as whom you marry to whether you let your first child live rather than bury it alive, down to the minor ones, like how you bathe or how far you stand from the person you are conversing with, all are predetermined by culture."[6]

Some aspects of culture are written; the majority are not. The traits of one's culture are learned in the process of living in that particular society. The process by which one acquires the rules of his or her cultural context is called by anthropologists enculturation and socialization by sociologists.

Through the processes of child training and education, a person comes to internalize the acceptable ways of living in his culture.

One of anthropology's important contributions to missionary strategy relates to cultivating a recognition of cultures as an integrated system. The anthropologically trained missionary more easily recognizes cultural factors and realizes that change in one area of this complex, integrated whole will of necessity have implications in other areas. Change in religion will often affect social structure, family relations, or eating practices. Recognizing culture helps missionary strategy bend to the needs of the various cultures of the world. One can effectively minister to a people only when he or she is familiar with the cultural patterns, knows the implications of culture, and perceives the nature of culture change.

Respecting Culture

Cultural understanding likewise helps missionaries respect culture. Cultures, like snowflakes, are both similar and different. Every culture provides for meeting the basic biological and psychological needs of people in their environment.[7]

Anthropology teaches that each culture should be judged on its own adaptive merit and respected as one way of adjusting to environment. This idea of respecting culture is spoken of as cultural relativism, or the practice of interpreting and evaluating behavior, belief, and objects in line with the standards and values of the culture to which those behaviors, beliefs, and objects belong. Cultural relativity understands that chopsticks, fingers, and forks (held either in the right hand or the left) are equally adaptive for getting food to the mouth. One of these adaptations is neither more advanced nor more ethical than another.

Accepting the concept of cultural relativism, and therefore more openly respecting a culture, does not involve abandoning either biblical or natural principle. Cultural relativity differs drastically from ethical relativity, which declares that any belief, practice, or adaptation is acceptable. Principles, especially biblical principles, can be maintained while holding cultural relativism.

A missionary, working with "swinging singles" in the United States, would not accept narcotic use or sexual permissiveness as just their cultural ways. On the basis of biblical absolutes, the missionary seeks to help people change to more acceptable patterns.

On the other hand, the missionaries to interior Dyaks in Kalimantan

(Borneo) would not of necessity insist that the Dyak women adopt Western dress in the form of blouses. Some Dyak cultures prescribe no clothing above the waist for women. Cultural relativism sees this form of dress as morally neutral and respects the cultural adaptation in line with the culture's own standard.

Anthropology helps the missionary respect culture by showing that many cultural factors are relative. Thus, the missionary can avoid two of the chief barriers to genuine identification, prejudice and ethnocentrism.

Identifying Various Cultures

Respecting culture helps missionaries identify various cultures within the area of his/her service. This identification of cultures is one of the most important tasks in planning missionary strategy. Political boundaries often have little to do with cultural boundaries. Several distinct cultures may exist within one political entity—such as the Yuraba, the Ibo, and the Higi cultures in the nation of Nigeria.

Even in a highly homogeneous society, where dress, language, and other factors are much the same, socio-economic factors may produce what is basically different cultural groupings. The upper middle class in the United States holds a culture basically different from the lower socio-economic groups. Failure to recognize the differences in groups in the United States, and other more developed countries, partly explains the church's inability to reach some groups.

Missionary strategy must recognize and take account of the difference in cultures. Peter Wagner suggests that the assumption that all people living in a certain region share the same culture has been a major obstacle to effective missionary strategy.[8] Thus, behavioral science, by helping identify various cultures, aids in the development of missionary strategy.

Learning About Culture

The study of behavioral science also contributes to the understanding of these various cultures through the many studies that have been provided by anthropologists. While significant insight is grained from books on anthropological theory and methodology, some of the most helpful material lies in studies of individual cultures. Such studies provide insights into the peoples—their worldview, histories, social structures, mythologies, material cultures and other facets of their culture. Cross-cultural workers should take advantage of these insights.

Actually living in a culture provides the most adequate opportunity for studying that culture. Learning through living in a culture is enhanced by anthropological insight as one trained in the discipline more clearly observes and more quickly understands. The cultural learning can be furthered and hastened by attention to the literature on the cultures. Peter Wagner indicates that reading an anthropolotical study of Latin American culture provided him insight into the people he had not achieved even though living in the culture.[9]

Identifying with Culture

Knowledge about culture, while extremely important, remains less important to missionary effectiveness than identifying with a culture. Identification with a culture involves being in actual, personal contact. It involves accepting and being accepted. It goes beyond merely adopting food, clothing, or housing similarities with the people. Identification means one understands, respects, loves, and serves the people in the culture. Barriers of personal relationship have been torn down and avenues of personal encounter opened.[10]

Two major deterents to missionary effectiveness, prejudice and ethnocentrism, must be overcome in order to identify with a culture. Prejudice leads one to believe that one group or kind of people is by nature inferior and that another group (usually one's own group) is inherently superior. Prejudice causes one to decide on the character, ability, worth, or intelligence of a person strictly on the basis of the racial, ethnic, or group to which that person belongs. When Nathanael asked, "Can any good thing come out of Nazareth?" (John 1:46, NASB), he was revealing prejudice. In his mind, all persons from Nazareth were inferior. The Nazi tragedy against the Jewish people was an example of prejudice in action.

Ethnocentrism leads one to accept the ways and values of his or her own culture as the standard. Whatever deviates from one's own ways of doing is wrong, backward, quaint, or defective. The missionary who rejects the food of the culture in which he or she serves may well be the victim of ethnocentrism. The Christian who mimics the language or makes fun of characteristics of a particular group is exhibiting ethnocentrism—subtly saying, "My group is superior."

Both prejudice and ethnocentrism block identification with and effectiveness within a culture. People resent rejection; they respond to acceptance. Understanding a culture helps the missionary avoid prejudice and ethnocentrism. Avoiding these negative attitudes contributes to the ability to identify with a culture.

The noblest example of identification remains he who "became flesh and dwelt among us" (John 1:1-4). The Incarnation is for all time the foremost model for missionary endeavor.[11] The missionary seeks in a human way to follow the example of Jesus in identification. The recognition of and the respect for culture that can come through behavioral science study enhances mission identification with culture.

Conclusion

The first contribution of behavioral science study is, therefore, an understanding of culture in general and of given cultures in particular. The behavioral sciences provide the tools for reaching the basic cultural understanding that is imperative both for missionary strategy and effectiveness.

Aiding Communication Processes

A second contribution of behavioral science lies in the area of aiding the process of effective communication. Eugene A. Nida, a well-known missionary anthropologist, insists that the primary contribution of cultural anthropology to missionary science is the provision of an effective communication process.[12] Cultural understanding contributes both to verbal and nonverbal communication patterns. The relevance of the gospel message can be demonstrated more clearly by one who understands the felt-needs of the people in a culture.

John Beekman contends that missionaries need to understand culture so as to select the scriptural truths that the people will recognize as having the greatest relevance to their lives. The most effective communication, he says, takes into account the beliefs and fears of the people. Beekman attributes the rapid growth of the gospel among the Chol Indians of Mexico to a culturally relevant witness that showed how the gospel met the people's needs for freedom of fear of the witch doctors and the relief of dread of sickness caused by sorcery.[13]

Expression

Behavioral science helps in expressing the message in a way that communicates clearly. Anthropology contributes to the effective translation of the message into the people's language. The concept of "dynamic equivalence" translation consists of striving for the impact and thought rather than simply formal correspondence of words. This concept enhances the communication of the real message. For the Indonesian, a literal translation of "kill two birds with one stone" would have little meaning. However, the Indonesian proverb which translated literally into English says, "While swimming, drink water" exactly and culturally expresses the American idiom in Indonesian thought patterns. In Irian Barat (New Guinea) the primary food is sweet potato. Dynamic equivalence would express the prayer Jesus taught the disciples, "Give us this day our daily sweet potato." Missionaries must seek dynamic equivalence in both translation and other expressions of the message.

Avoiding Miscommunication

Cultural insights aid also in avoiding miscommunication. It is easy for one in a culture different from his/her own to give the wrong idea either by the spoken word or nonverbal patterns. The missionary might decline food on the basis that the people need the food far more than he or she. To the missionary the rejection would be humanitarian. To the national the refusal of food might be either a rejection of the culture or the person and lead to a serious loss of face. In most Western cultures the gesture "thumbs up" expresses approval but in some cultures the same gesture has an unwholesome meaning. Standing very close to another while talking indicates close relationship in some cultures—rudeness in others. The culturally aware missionary uses cultural insights to avoid unnecessary misunderstanding.

Aid in understanding communication comprises one of the more helpful areas of behavioral science to the missionary task. A culturally relevant witness usually demands a culturally aware communicator. The enhancement of communication remains a major contribution of behavioral science.

Dealing with Personal Adjustment

A third contribution of behavioral science relates to helping the missionary adjust personally to a new culture. Every cross-cultural worker must deal with his or her own reaction to the culture of the people among whom he/she serves. This demanding adjustment can be made easier or harder according to preparation, insight, and to some degree, determination. The unfamiliar in the new culture leads to reactions that may cause either stress and rejection or aid empathy and acceptance. The study of cultural anthropology contributes directly to proper personal accommodation.

Two major problems are associated with personal adjustment, cultural shock and cultural overhang. This section describes these related problem areas and suggests how anthropology can help in solving these problems related to personal adjustment.

Culture Shock

The necessity of learning a new set of cultural rules can be, and usually is, a traumatic experience. The anxiety that results from facing new and unfamiliar sights, smells, tastes, ways of behaving, values, and patterns of thinking are called "culture jolts" by Louis J. Luzbetak.[14] These culture jolts produce not only anxiety but frustration and perplexities. Missionaries often wonder, *Why was my action or words misunderstood?* Unsuccessful adjustment to culture jolts leads to the syndrome of culture shock. Persons entering a new culture usually experience culture shock to some degree. Most will deal with the newness and begin to adjust. Some will allow culture shock to push them toward rejection and either failure or lessened effectiveness as a missionary.

The process of culture shock involves several stages. The fascination or tourist stage allows one to experience the new culture as an exciting, interesting place. There is a tendency to idealize the new culture. This stage is revealed in many new missionary newsletters.

The missionary who stays in the new culture often finds this early fascination changing to resentment and even rejection. Rules of behavior, expression, and belief that he/she has held for years are being threatened. New ways seem inferior, unwise, unproductive, or actually wrong. In time this attitude of resentment may lead to withdrawal. The one experiencing culture shock may well stay away from the new ways, foods, smells, and so forth. In time the same rejection begins to apply to people. Culture shock can even create a spirit of animosity toward nationals and indigenous ways.

This stage of culture shock is often accompanied by the idealization of the familiar and a craving for one's own ways, the homeland, and its cultural practices. Homesickness, overly critical attitudes of the new culture, derogatory remarks directed to the people and their ways, and rejection of the host culture all reveal a developing problem of culture shock.

The extreme stage of culture shock leads to depression and total rejection of the new culture. At this point the one in shock may well either follow the course of complete rejection of the new culture and return to the familiar, or go native. Going native involves renouncing the former ways and values and indiscriminately adopting the ways and values of the new culture. Luzbetak points out that going native is not true identification but an improper adjustment usually caused by a desire for merit or acceptance.[15] Going native may well be a reaction to feelings of guilt brought on by what the missionary recognizes as rejection of the culture.

The final stage of the culture shock process is recovery. The missionary learns some of the new rules. He begins to be more comfortable, learning to communicate, to accept, to be accepted, seeing cultural traits as learned ways of reacting and no longer rejects those who practice them. After a time, he/she sees the meaning and use for some of the traits. The missionary in the tropics, for example, finds that the afternoon rest is a necessity for continued health rather than an evidence of laziness. A missionary learns that bride price is not buying the woman but a cultural device for giving stability to marriage.

The goal of adjusting to culture is the achievement of empathy, acceptance, and identification with culture. The ability to communicate, accept, and serve depends to a large extent on one's successful adjustment to culture shock. As one sees, understands, and accepts the new culture, the ability to serve is enhanced.

Culture shock can be minimized by attention to the following procedures:

1. Seek to understand the "whys of cultural practices." Avoid comparing cultural practice with your homeland. Notice the functions of various culture traits.
2. Move to or join the new environment. Do not attempt to transplant home to the new land. Develop a taste for indigenous food; use local transportation; visit local entertainment.
3. Learn to communicate. This involves both verbal and nonverbal communication patterns. Pay attention to gestures, mannerisms, and the like. Be willing to talk, make mistakes, and try again.
4. Develop friendships with nationals from various strata of the society. Guard against the tendency to associate only with one group (the wealthy or some minority). Accept the peculiarities of people in the culture.
5. Enter into the life flow of the culture. Visit the markets. Refrain from overdependence on household help. Allow children to form friendships in the community. Investigate the possibilities of missionary children attending local schools and perhaps the missionary also could attend.
6. Avoid strict association with other missionaries. The mission com-

pound or station makes proper identification difficult if not impossible. Cultivate association with both Christian and non-Christian nationals. As a missionary you are in the new culture on a redemptive mission. This redemptive mission is more important than comfort or personal convenience. Putting the purpose first helps one deal with culture shock.

Cultural anthropology helps the missionary deal with culture shock by gaining the ability to understand and respect the host culture. These insights provide perspective for more adequate identification. Eating dog meat is not wrong, backward, nor injurious. Anthropology helps the missionary learn what is most important and thereby deal with culture shock.

Cultural Overhang

Cultural overhang, a second culture-related problem leads missionaries to insist that those in other cultures deny their set rules and adopt the missionary's ways. This problem area leads missionaries not only to maintain their standards of church life, cleanliness, punctuality, morality, dress, or value systems, but to insist that locals do the same. Peter Wagner calls cultural overhang an example of a missionary "creator complex," that is, the desire to make a people over in the missionary's image.[16]

One expression of cultural overhang, paternalism, causes the missionary to treat nationals more or less as children. Paternalism usually reveals an attitude of superiority and "we know best," leading missionaries to fail to recognize the people in the culture as adults and refuse to honor their thoughts and ideas.

Paternalism is one of the most damaging attitudes with respect to missionary-national relations. It not only blocks genuine fellowship but deprives the workers of valuable insights the nationals could provide. Furthermore, the missionary is likely to introduce and insist on an expression of Christianity and church life foreign to the people.

The same efforts that alleviate culture shock can help overcome cultural overhang. Anthropology, by showing the function of various cultural traits in the society, can help the missionary accept local ways. Respect for culture helps missionaries accept local adults as leaders and advisors. Overcoming ethnocentrism to a marked degree helps solve the problem of cultural overhang.

Conclusion

Cultural shock and cultural overhang remain two barriers to authentic identification and effective ministry. Missionaries must learn to bend strategy and life-style to culture, thereby enhancing their ministry. Few efforts are more needed or more rewarding than successfully achieving proper personal adjustment to the new culture.

Achieving Accommodation Without Syncretism

The goal of Christian missions is responsible, reproducing believers in responsible, reproducing congregations. This goal is best reached when indigenous churches are planted and grow naturally in the new soil (see ch. 3). Cultural anthropology contributes significantly to accommodation, that is, adjusting church life and Christian life-style to culture and to the avoidance of syncretism, that is, the mixture of Christian truth and life-style with non-Christian elements.

Understanding Accommodation

Accommodation may be defined as the respectful, prudent, scientifically and theologically proper adjustment of the Church (church) and the Christian life to the indigenous culture in attitude, action, and basic approach.[17] The purposes of accommodation include allowing the people to develop their own expression of Christian theology, living, and church life, as well as to increase missionary effectiveness. Moreover, the object of accommodation is to achieve an indigenous church in the fullest sense of the word (see ch. 3).

The importance of accommodation can hardly be overstated. Care must be taken, however, in that the methods of accommodation are acceptable and the limits observed. Donald A McGavran has helped set the stage for proper accommodation in his discussion of the "four Christianities."[18]

McGavran sees Christianity One, or Theological Christianity, as comprising beliefs about God, man, sin, salvation, Scripture, eternal life, and right or wrong. These beliefs are based on biblical revelation and, though varying slightly from denomination to denomination, must remain unchanged in all cultures. Accommodation does not allow nonbiblical aspects to develop. Theological error should not be allowed in order to make Christianity more acceptable to the new culture.

Christianity Two, or Ethical Christianity, includes the applied value systems which Christians ought to do under various circumstances. Christians are to honor their father and mother in every culture, but how this honor is expressed will be defined somewhat differently in various cultures. In some cultures, accepting anything with the left hand is rude, while the same action in other societies has no negative meaning.

Accommodation can be achieved in Christianity Two. So long as the biblical principle is maintained, a cultural expression is acceptable. Paul's teaching regarding the length of hair for men and women (1 Cor. 11:1-12) sets a principle of dressing and grooming so as to give an accurate view of character. In most cultures today, so long as the principle of modesty is observed, the actual length of hair is of little importance. If, however, in a given area, long hair should convey the idea of a lack of moral value or rebellion, Christians would not wear long hair.

Christianity Three, or Ecclesiastical Christianity, includes church customs, ways of worship, forms of prayer, styles of church buildings, meeting times, and types of organization. These customs can vary greatly from culture to culture. In a highly literate culture, worship once a week may be sufficient. Daily worship after the evening meal may be more effective in a nonliterate society. Times of worship, days of worship and styles of worship may vary according to the needs of the culture. Accommodation allows great latitude in changing church customs to fit culture.

A major aspect of Church custom relates to leadership patterns. Cultures that honor age may have difficulty accepting the young, trained leader felt necessary by the missionary. In such cases, leadership can sometimes be given to the older men while the preaching and teaching is done by the younger who can read.

Christianity Four, or Customary Christianity, involves local customs followed by Christians. This body of customs relates to food, dress, and ordinary ways of living. Accommodation is needed here to avoid the Christians "going Western." Early Christians in one area of Java were called "Javanese who wear shoes and hats" because the church leader insisted that Christians adopt Dutch clothing.[19] Accommodation is most valid for Christianity Four.

Accommodation, then, adjusts to customs, language, and styles but guards against mixing Christianity with nonbiblical ideas. Anthropology can help the missionary know how to introduce necessary changes and how to encourage churches and Christians to fit into their own culture.

Grunlan and Mayers suggest four questions that can guide the missionary in accommodating to culture.

1. What is the norm in this culture? That is, what should a person do in this situation if he is to act as a responsible member of this culture?
2. Is the behavior in keeping with the cultural norm? Is the behavior that of a responsible member of the culture?
3. Does the cultural norm need changing? Is the cultural norm in conflict with a biblical principle? Care needs to be taken on this point to make sure we are evaluating the cultural norm by biblical standards and not by our own cultural norms. Even if our own cultural norms are in line with the biblical principles, that does not mean that the other culture's norms are not just because they differ from ours. A principle may take a different form in a different culture.
4. Who is responsible for changing the norm? If it is discovered that the norm in a given culture is not in keeping with the biblical principles, then who is responsible for bringing about the change? Not the missionary, but the nationals as they are guided by the Holy Spirit. The change may or may not be that which the missionary would have done, but it will be in keeping with both the biblical principle and the culture if it is Spirit-directed.[20]

Avoiding Syncretism

Christianity necessarily, properly, and ceaselessly adjusts to cultures. In the process of achieving these adjustments, erroneous decisions can be and have been made. Such errors in accommodation lead to a major missionary problem, syncretism.

Syncretism has been defined "as the union of two opposite forces, beliefs, systems or tenents so that the united form is a new thing, neither one nor the other."[21] A. R. Tippett mentions two kinds of mixtures that might be called syncretism. One mixture involves the distortion of Christian teaching by mixing it with nonChristian myth. The second mixture involves the singing of Western, Calvinistic theology in an unfamiliar chant to a drumbeat previously used for a pagan dance.

These two mixtures are different. The difference led Tippett to employ the term, "Christopaganism" for the first mixture. Tippett goes on to show how in the thinking of a Latin American Indian, Juan, animistic myths were so intertwined with elements of the Bible that the biblical account became distorted. Juan, who considered himself a normal Christian, showed his animistic mixture as he related his understanding and his syncretism of the biblical message and animistic myth.

> He tells us that the Savior watches over people on the road. He died on a cross to save the wayfarer from the Jews, whom he equates with devils, and who were supposedly cannibalistic. Originally the sun was as cold as the moon, but it grew warmer when the Holy Child was born. He was the son of a virgin among the Jews, who sent her away because they knew the Child would bring light. St. Joseph took her to Bethelehm where the Child was born. The sun grew warmer and the day brighter. The demons ran away and hid in the mountain ravines. Their activity is confined to night because the Savior watches over the day, for the sun is the eye of God. After three days the Holy Child started work as a carpenter. He made a door from a log. The log was too short so he stretched it out like a rope to the required length. Fearing him the people determined to kill him and the family fled from village to village across the mountains. In one village he planted a cornfield. The people were bitten by a swarm of flies. The Savior said, "Don't eat them, eat me instead." He visited the afterworld and then they nailed him to a cross so the people would remember that demons would be punished and would stop eating people.[22]

Such mixing of biblical truth with nonChristian myth is unacceptable and in no wise proper accommodation.

McGavran points to Deism as an example of improper adjustment of Christianity to culture. The deist culture placed the laws of life and world in first place. Deism did not so much ban God as it relegated him to an absentee deity who had created the world and left it in control of natural law. The laws, not God, governed the world. Miracles were impossible. Prayer was meditation influencing only the one who prayed.

In attempting to adjust Christianity to deist culture, McGavran declares, the adjustments all but destroyed the biblical faith. He says:

> Under the guise of adjusting Christianity to a rational culture, theologians and leaders of these segments of the church gave birth to a new syncretistic religion. They still called it Christianity. It used the old familiar words. It met in church houses and listened to robed choirs. It sang hymns and employed ministers trained in seminaries which devoted themselves to hastening the adjustment to deistic culture. It looked very like Christianity—but it radically disbelieved the Bible, had very little faith in the resurrection of our Lord and had little power. It converted few sinners. In America, it maintained itself by proselytizing out of the orthodox churches Christians whose faith had grown cold. It emphasized ethics—partly because righteousness was the one component of the pure faith in which it yet believed, and partly because, having lost the vertical dimension, it had to compensate by stressing the horizontal. Missiologists do not have to go abroad to observe the tragic futility of syncretism.[22]

Mission strategy, in the effort to accommodate to culture, must guard against syncretism. The essential biblical message cannot and must not be changed by missionary accommodation adjustments to culture. It will remain in harmony with biblical teachings while at the same time couched in terms understandable and meaningful to the host culture. The proper formulation may not be pleasing to the culture but should be understandable and meaningful. The limit of accommodation is reached before syncretism becomes a reality.

Proper Accommodation

Proper strategy seeks accommodation, making the message relevant and easily accepted by the people in the receptor culture. Accommodation involves both identification and cummunication. While guarding against syncretism, accommodation strives for indigenous Christian thinking and church life.

Two important strategies, meeting felt needs and using functional substitutes, aid the process of proper accommodation. Meeting felt needs shows the people that the message is relevant. The missionary seeks to communicate the gospel in ways that cause the people themselves to recognize their need. To advocate change when the people do not perceive the change as in any way relating to their needs is to attain little or no innovation or change.

The wise missionary discovers the felt needs of the people. These felt needs may include such things as reaching freedom from the fear of the shaman, or overcoming the terror of sickness, or finding ways to achieve family peace and harmony. Different peoples have different sets of felt needs.

Once the felt needs of the people are understood, the messenger can communicate to the people how the message meets those needs. Response to the gospel becomes less difficult when the people see how the gospel meets their perceived needs. Too many Christian messengers communicate those aspects of the gospel which interest them rather than applying the gospel to the felt needs of the people.

Accommodation allows local, indigenous ways their fullest expression. There are, however, some practices and beliefs that are incompatible with biblical teachings. Accommodation does not perpetuate unChristian, unbiblical factors in the name of adjustment to culture. Change is often necessary.

When change is necessary the missionary must remember that he/she can never enact the change but only advocate it. The innovator, or changer, must be from within the culture itself. The missionary can serve as a helper in the change process.

One helpful strategy in achieving the change is that of providing functional substitutes. A functional substitute is a cultural element introduced to replace a cultural element that must be eliminated or drastically changed in the process of a group's following Christ. To fail to provide functional substitutes opens the door for reversion or syncretism.

In Java a Muslim farmer sacrifices to the field spirits, seeking protection for his crop. When asked why, if there is one God, a Muslim would placate field spirits, the farmer would likely answer "God is a great God, concerned with great things like building mosques and holy wars. God does not have time," says the farmer, "to care for the crops in one little field. That is the job of the field spirits."

Should this Muslim farmer become a Christian, the sacrifice to the field spirits could not be continued. Every Christian in all cultures must heed, "Thou shalt have no other gods before me." To simply prohibit the ceremony of sacrifice to field spirits would leave a serious cultural void. Better to provide a Christian ceremony with prayer to God for protection of the fields. This ceremony would be a functional substitute.

Functional substitutes then meet the cultural needs without perpetuating unbiblical rituals or patterns. Any effort at accommodation must seek to provide valid, satisfying, functional substitutes. Only when these cultural factors are in place can accommodation without syncretism be attained.

Proper accommodation is one of the most demanding, creative and profitable of all missionary efforts. Balanced church growth is enhanced by proper accommodation.

Conclusion

Effective missionaries should make full use of the insights and teachings of cultural anthropology and sociology. These disciplines are simply tools—but important tools—for all engaged in cross-cultural evangelism and church ministry. Rather than fearing or rejecting the behavioral sciences, missionary strategy should make full use of these insights.

Questions and Activities

1. What is the difference in cultural relativism and ethical relativity?
2. How do culture jolts lead to culture shock? How can missionaries overcome culture shock?
3. Describe the difference between accommodation and syncretism. Use illustrations.
4. Read a description of a culture. Suggest how a Christian movement could be accommodated to this culture. What felt needs do you think would be present? What functional substitutes might be employed?

Further Reading

Grunlan, Stephen A., and Mayers, Marvin K. *Cultural Anthropology: A Christian Perspective* (Zondervan)

McGavran, Donald A. *The Clash Between Christianity and Culture* (Canon)

Kraft, Charles H. "Dynamic Equivalence Churches," *Missiology* 1 (1973):36-57.

Smalley, William A. *Readings in Missionary Anthropology* II (William Carey Library)

Luzbetak, Louis J. *The Church and Culture* (Divine Word Publication)

Notes

1. Donald A. McGavran, *Understanding Church Growth,* p. 207.

2. Donald A. McGavran and Winfield C. Arn, *Ten Steps for Church Growth* (San Francisco: Harper & Row, Publishers, 1977), p. 26.

3. Eugene Nida, *Customs and Cultures* (New York: Harper & Brothers, 1954), p. xi-xii.

4. Louis J. Luzbetak, *The Church and Cultures* (Techny, Ill.: Divine Word Publications, 1970), pp. 3-4.

5. Alan R. Tippett, "Anthropology: Luxury or Necessity for Missions," *Evangelical Mission Quarterly* 1 (1968):7-19.

6. C. Peter Wagner, *Frontiers of Mission Strategy,* p. 88.

7. See Stephen A. Grunlan and Marvin K. Mayers, *Cultural Anthropology: A Christian Perspective* (Grand Rapids: Zondervan, 1979), p. 43.

8. Wagner, *Frontiers of Missionary Strategy,* pp. 89-90.

9. Ibid., pp. 88-89.

10. Ibid., p. 96.

11. Charles H. Kraft, "God's Model for Cross-Cultural Communication—the Incarnation," *Evangelical Missions Quarterly* 9 (1973):205-16; Kraft, "The Incarna-

tion, Cross-Cultural Communication and Communication Theory," *Evangelical Missionary Quarterly* 9 (1973):277-84.

12. Eugene A. Nida, "The Role of Anthropology in Christian Missions," *Practical Anthropology* 6, 3(1959):310.

13. John Beekman, "A Culturally Relevant Witness," *Practical Anthropology* 4, 6(1957):83-88.

14. Luzbetak, pp. 84-90.

15. Ibid., p. 99.

16. Wagner, *Frontiers of Missionary Strategy,* p. 97.

17. Luzbetak, p. 341.

18. Donald A. McGavran. *The Clash Between Christianity and Culture* (Washington, D.C.: Canon, 1974)), pp. 45-49.

19. Ebbie C. Smith, *God's Miracles: Indonesian Church Growth,* p. 102.

20. Grunlan and Mayers, pp. 30-31.

21. Alan R. Tippett, "Christopaganism or Indigenous Christianity," in *Christopaganism or Indigenous Christianity,* ed. Tetsunai Yamamori and Charles R. Tabor (South Pasadena, Calif.: William Carey Library, 1975), p. 17.

22. Ibid., pp. 21-22.

23. Ibid., pp. 47-48.

6
Overcoming Obstacles to Church Growth

Church growth is imperative! God wills it! Christians want it! Churches expect it! The world needs it! The Kingdom awaits it! The Spirit will empower it! In spite of its importance church growth is often hindered by a variety of obstacles. Those concerned about church growth must be aware of these obstacles and ways to overcome them. Obstacles to church growth can be grouped under theological, ecclesiastical, methodological, and spiritual obstacles.

Theological Obstacles

Beliefs concerning God, revelation, sin, conversion, the church and its mission, eternal states, and Christian responsibility remain central for missions and church growth. Deviation from the biblical foundation of these or other biblical doctrines render church growth improbable at least, impossible in most cases. Theological confusion constitutes a major obstacle to church growth and must be faced and overcome if growth is expected. Of the many theological misunderstandings that can hinder church growth, two will be discussed—universalism and humanitarianism.

Overcoming the Obstacle of Universalism

Universalism, the belief that all people finally will be brought to salvation, renders Great Commission missions unnecessary. This erroneous belief leads to mission methods that stress dialogue without efforts for conversion, presence without any call for decision, and service with no view toward salvation. Certainly Harold Lindsell correctly says that

> Universalism cuts the nerve of missions. If all men are to be redeemed at last, it makes little difference whether the gospel is or is not to be preached to all men during this age.[1]

The beliefs connected with universalism are varied but mostly rest on two concepts, that is, the love of God that will bring all men to final salvation and reliance on scientific knowledge rather than revelation. Against these views, Great Commission missions understands the necessity for conversion missions based on the lostness of mankind apart from Christ. Universalism opposes the truth of biblical authority and bases the approach on mankind's needs and possibilities.

A major problem related to universalism lies in the area of the approach to other religions. Universalism tends to see good in other religions and approaches them by means of dialogue rather than witness. To be sure, there are noble teachings in Islam, Hinduism, and other religions. Further, it is true that approach should be made to persons who follow other faiths. Christian missions, however, must never overlook the truth that "there is salvation in no one else" (Acts 4:12, NASB).

Universalism and church growth are mutually exclusive. Therefore, universalism stands as a major obstacle. How then can universalism and the methods that accompany it be overcome?

Recommitment to the biblical teachings such as the nature of mankind and redemption, and acceptance of the commands of the Great Commission erase some of the major errors of universalism. Mankind is bound under the power of Satan and can only be freed through the greater power of God's redemptive plan in Christ. This decisive struggle of two powers is at the heart of genuine missionary activity and church growth efforts.

Thus, Great Commission missions must call forth a decision. Since the power of Satan over mankind can only be broken through the greater power of God's redemption, missions as mere presence or dialogue is forever inadequate. Service projects alone leave the lost bound under Satan's power. Missions with no authoritative call for repentance remains an unbiblical and therefore invalid approach.

The proclaimer of the gospel heralds the message of the Lord himself. Tippett defends the missionary who calls for decision, saying:

> Men have to be persuaded to become Christian by their own positive choice, and the validity of the conversion depends on the fact that they have made a right-decision of their own volition. The monological dogmatism, so frequently criticised, is not the dogmatism of the missionary, but the proclamation. . . . The dialogical writers have completely missed the point that the proclamation comes, not from the herald, but from God.[2]

The obstacle of universalism can be defeated only by this return to the biblical truth of redemption and its priority. Church growth rests on the theological foundation of man's need and God's provision. Missions without a call for decision is missions without church growth.

Humanitarianism

Humanitarianism, the theology that places meeting social needs, overcoming oppression and injustice, and bettering living conditions as *the primary* goal of missions, obstructs church growth. The opposite tendency, to conceive of the social aspects of the gospel less than a vital part of the faith, likewise destroys any chance of balanced, genuine growth. As seen in chapter 2, nowhere is balance more imperative than in the arena of the relationship of evangelization and social involvement.

Christianity's social aspect is a vital and indispensable part of the church's (and churches') ministry. Any neglect of or failure to fully implement the biblical charges to relieve suffering, overthrow oppression, correct injustice, and improve life falls short of orthodox Christianity.

Church Growth efforts must accept and realize that the Church is called to serve as the Church and this call includes social ministry and action. Evangelistic and social mandates remain in proper perspective only as the following suggestions are observed.

First, maintain an evangelistic priority. Refuse to allow either the emphasis on discipleship or social involvement to cloud the evangelistic imperative. To neglect evangelism in order to either disciple or lift socially, ultimately leads to inability to serve because of loss of power.

Secondly, maintain the social priority. Recognize and implement this part of the biblical mandate to the Christian movement. Practice a wholistic approach.

Thirdly, separate a portion of the churches' resources for both social ministry and action. Relieve those who suffer. Attempt also to change the society that injures people.

Fourthly, keep the proper balance by adjusting the level of involvement to the local situation. In some cases, the social may consume more of the church's energy than in others. In few, if any, cases should the social be primary. Should extreme cases demand more social attention (disasters, extreme oppression, etc.) the church must return as soon as possible to the priority of evangelism.

Finally, never allow either evangelism or social involvement to be totally eclipsed. Both should be sought in some proportion at all times.

Humanitarianism is a part of the gospel. It obstructs Church Growth only when allowed to grow out of balance. Properly balanced, social involvement stimulates growth. Church Growth must joyfully accept and energetically attempt both the social as well as the evangelistic mandate.

Conclusion

Theological soundness enhances church growth. Any deviation from revelational truth stands in the way of increasing disciples and congregations. Correcting theological error helps eliminate some of the obstacles that hinder church growth.

Methodological Obstacles

Church growth can also be inhibited by obstacles springing from faulty methods. This is not to say that growth depends on methods alone. The Spirit can, as I have said, grant growth in spite of methodology. Still, faulty methods do at times stand in the way of the most adequate growth. In this chapter I will discuss four representative methodological errors—gradualism, perfectionism, equalitarianism, and paternalism.

Gradualism

Gradualism, a methodological error, continues seedsowing activities designed to prepare for later harvest when harvesting is possible. Gradualism performs service now in order that church growth may occur *later.* Good deeds, including medical, educational, training, cultural activities, are carried out in anticipation that these activities will lead to a later harvest. As McGavran says, "We are not perturbed when it (gradualism) is really the only possible way: we are perturbed when it is unnecessary."[3] When circumstances render *only* preparation possible, then, certainly, that method is dictated. Gradualism stands in the way of growth when harvest awaits but the missionaries and churches continue seed-sowing rather than ingathering.

Overcoming gradualism is possible though not necessarily easy. One method consists of recognizing it and accepting the possibility of harvest. Often, a mission or church is so imprisoned by the traditional ways that new methods are not considered. Harvest can often be furthered by exchanging the reaper for the planter.

To change from gradualism to harvest may require directing the major witness to another and more responsive segment of the population. A tragedy in missionary strategy occurs when witness is restricted to a resistant population when receptive peoples are present and waiting. If Missions continue to work among the more resistant "classes" while responsive "masses" go unevangelized, gradualism prevails. "We will win the upper classes," say missionaries, "and they will then reap the harvest among the masses." Winning the upper classes sometimes demands long cultivation with little harvest. When witnesses turn to the masses, growth will often become a reality.

Awareness of possibility for growth and commitment to growth remain the primary ingredients of a plan to overcome gradualism. Whitened harvest must be reaped. Methods should be linked to possibilities of growth. Gradualism, when harvest awaits, should be set aside and efforts to disciple people and plant churches instituted.

Perfectionism

Nowhere is balance more necessary than in the area of evangelizing and discipling (discipling and perfecting). Churches are constantly pushed to the imperative task of shepherding, developing, and caring for the Christians and in perfecting the church itself. This is the discipling or perfecting role. Churches likewise must acknowledge and act on the responsibility to evangelize all mankind.

Overemphasizing the discipling or perfecting function can easily become an obstacle to church growth. When churches neglect evangelizing in order to disciple or perfect, church growth will decline. Unfortunately, there is a tendency for churches to neglect evangelizing in the drive to build up members and meet the churches' own needs.

Perfectionism hinders church growth in three main ways. First, effort, people, and resources are poured into the perfecting effort and pulled out of the evangelizing ministry. While the importance of perfecting can never be minimized, the priority of evangelizing must not be overlooked. McGavran rightly says, "during period of expansion when the Faith is surging forward in some population, if any part of the task must suffer it should be perfecting."[4] Failure to properly prioritize evangelism hinders church growth.

Perfectionism, in the second place, hinders church growth when Christians and churches so center on spiritual experience or renewal that outreach suffers. Church renewal efforts and certain charismatic experiences easily fall into the danger of emphasizing fellowship, spiritual exercises, and warm worship experiences and neglecting evangelistic outreach. The error of seeking growth as better without seeking growth as bigger or broader is a danger to church growth. There can even be an attitude of greater concern to draw other Christians into the deeper life than to bring lost persons to the Lord.

The drive to perfect can also lead Christians and churches to neglect relationship with both nonChristians and new Christians. As Christians mature they sometimes develop a lack of patience with and feeling for those on a lower spiritual plane or those who are not believers. This lack of true identification with the spiritually needy adversely affects church growth.

The problem of perfectionism, while not easily answered, can be overcome. Commitment to evangelism and outreach remains the primary avenue for solving problems related to perfectionism. In addition, decisions must be reached as to how much "civilization" is required for salvation and church membership.

Balanced Church Growth demands that both efforts toward evangelism and perfection (discipling) be properly emphasized. As with brotherhood (see chapter three) perfection is the fruit and salvation is the root. Perfectionism becomes an obstacle to true church growth when it is overemphasized—that is, when discipleship hinders evangelism.

Equalitarianism

Church growth is often obstructed by the administrative mistake of assigning equal resources to all fields. No field should be neglected. Responsive fields should, however, receive a greater proportion of resources—people and money. Equalitarianism assigns people and money on a "same-for-all" basis and fields awaiting harvest often go ungathered.

Approaching mission administration on a basis of the same resources for all areas also prevents Missions from responding quickly to developing opportunities. Sometimes an area suddenly turns receptive. The gospel begins to spread among some segment or segments of a population. Good missionary strategy demands that missionary resources be channeled quickly into a field where response is rising.

In one field, tremendous response arose among one segment of the population. Missionaries from over the entire area could have linguistically functioned among the responsive peoples. Mission policy, however, kept missionary resources locked to the less responsive areas and provided no increase among those clamoring to accept the message. Equalitarianism obstructs church growth by insisting on the same-for-all.

The problems of equalitarianism can be corrected by dedication to the principle of emphasizing evangelism among responsive peoples. Strategy and policy should be adjusted in order to take advantage of increasing receptivity. No missionary group should remain chained to unproductive work when more responsive fields lie unharvested. Resources should be placed in fields that are white to harvest without neglecting the fields where response has not yet borne fruit.

What then does church growth have for resistant peoples? Certainly not neglect. Church growth teaches that every person has not only the need but the right to hear the gospel. Missionary efforts must continue even where people are as hard as flint against the gospel.

Mission strategy continues contact with resistant peoples. Some will respond. Who knows but that the group will turn responsive and missions must be there to reap the harvest. The unresponsive are important to God and therefore to church growth.

What of those called to unresponsive fields? When God calls, God's people respond. God calls men and women to the unresponsive fields. When one is led to an unresponsive people, that one is judged by his or her faithfulness not his or her fruitfulness. Church growth affirms and supports those who serve among the unresponsive. Church growth only suggests that emphasis and effort be concentrated on the responding segments of mankind.

Equalitarianism also can be overcome by developing a task force to enter developing fields. Mission policy should allow moving of resources to these pockets of receptivity. When the purpose of missionary and evangelistic activity is clearly maintained, equalitarianism can be overcome and the hindrances it causes to church growth neutralized.

Paternalism

Paternalism, the tendency of the missionary or sponsoring group to assume a place of authority or undue influence on the developing church or Christians, severely obstructs church growth. Church leaders practicing paternalism tend to treat adults in the developing churches as children. This error is not restricted to foreign missions. Sponsoring churches and pastors as well as denominational workers in the United States can be overbearing to the point of severely restricting the development of a new church. Any time the missionaries or sponsoring groups insist on making the decisions, demanding compliance, controlling the funds, and in general remaining in charge, paternalism is present.

Paternalism stems partly from a sense of responsibility for the work and to those who are supporting it. Often, the reason for paternalism lies in the mistrust of the new Christians and their abilities to lead the church. Fear of doctrinal or denominational deviation produces paternalism. Still, the most basic source of paternalism remains the feeling of responsibility and/or the desire to be recognized. Thus, paternalism often hides under the cloak of accountability but is actually a desire for appreciation. The problem is, as Peter Wagner has said, "Paternalism will not bring a church to perfection."[5]

The problem of paternalism sometimes surfaces in the areas of money and subsidy. The missionary or sponsoring group who controls funds can easily slip into an attitude of authority and domination. Funds and other rewards are sometimes given to those who submit to the missionaries and withheld from those who do not. This is parternalism at its worst. Nowhere is paternalism more apparent or more destructive than in relation to subsidy. (See ch. 3.)

Paternalism obstructs church growth by limiting true communication between missionary and national or between sponsoring church and mission. This attitude denies the development of true cooperation, expresses most disturbingly the cultural overhang of the missionary, and most often adversely affects the development of new Christians and churches. Paternalistic methods, including subsidy, initially may seem easier to the missionary and sponsoring groups, but in the long run will prove detrimental to the very work they are attempting to help.

How can missionaries, sponsoring groups, and denominational workers overcome paternalism? Humility is the beginning point. Realizing that the local people are adults and committed Christians will help the missionary avoid the error of overcontrol and domination. Trust in the Holy Spirit also helps overthrow paternalistic tendencies. Believing that the Spirit can speak to and direct new Christians in new churches avoids the feeling of having to control and direct. Dedication to indigenous church strategies also allows missionaries to stand aside and let the local church become the local expression of Christianity.

Another help in overcoming paternalism stems from a relaxation of control from the home base. Often regulations from sending organizations force the missionary to accountability that makes trust and cooperation difficult if not impossible. Regulations from the sending body should be sufficiently broad to allow creative solutions to the problems of developing churches. The same rules for every area may make administrative sense but may also force workers to paternalism.

Paternalism must be overcome if new churches are to develop in healthy ways. Few obstacles obstruct balanced church growth more than paternalism. Overcoming this methodological error remains an imperative step in balanced church growth.

Conclusion

There are many methodological barriers to balanced church growth. A method that enhances growth in one area may hinder in another region. Methods must be examined and, if they prove obstructive, be changed for more productive patterns.

Ecclesiastical Obstacles

Other obstacles to church growth stem directly from matters related to Churches, congregations, and the ways in which they work. These obstacles are both theological and methodological but since they relate directly to the life and ministry of denominations and churches, they will be called ecclesiastical obstacles to church growth.

Union

Union or cooperation can obstruct rather than enhance church growth. Interdenominational cooperation is obviously a beneficial method. Union, the merging of denominations, often disrupts more than it helps. In church growth, as in other forms of church work, the goal is unity rather than union.

Peter Wagner suggests that while interchurch cooperation can stimulate church growth, what he calls "hyper-cooperation" can obstruct the discipling of people and developing of churches.[6] I agree with Wagner that interdenominational cooperation is a useful tool for social action, relief, education, fellowship, and enrichment. Such cooperation has not usually proved beneficial to evangelistic undertakings. I further agree that cooperation, while helpful, can be destructive and an obstacle to church growth when used for the wrong ends or allowed to develop imbalance.

Any effort toward union that results in one of the following aberations of church life will obstruct genuine growth. A distortion of the basic theological foundation of the deity of Christ, mankind's need for salvation, and the responsibility of Great Commission missions inhibits if not prevents balanced church growth. Doctrinal error hits at the very heart of the growth of churches. Union movements easily lead to watered-down doctrinal convictions and thus block growth.

A distortion of the evangelistic thrust of the Christian movement inhibits balanced growth. Because union movements are especially effective in social ministries, the tendency is to emphasize these social efforts. Social ministries constitute an imperative and normative fact of Christian ministry. An overemphasis on social ministry blocks balanced church growth.

Evangelistic emphasis can be distorted by the diverting of energy and resources from disciple-making to cooperative upkeep. As Lyle Schaller notes, the broader the cooperation the more complex the social relationships to hold it together. Thus, he says, time for "membership outreach" is limited.[7]

A distortion of the place of Christian mission and efforts to overcome injustice can inhibit church growth. As will be emphasized in the following section, justice and freedom are vital concerns for the Christian movement. Some cooperative movements have, however, placed such emphasis on seeking justice that disciple-making has been lost. I question the possibility of cooperation with some types of organizations without sacrificing church growth. When efforts for righting wrong turn Christians away from effective evangelism and balanced growth of Christians and churches, cooperation has turned obstructive.

Can the obstructions to growth brought on by union efforts be overcome? Yes, but not easily. Christians, denominations, and congregations must strenuously resist any cooperative effort that would lead to any compromise on such essential beliefs as the deity of Christ, the need of man, salvation by grace, and the necessity of Great Commission missions. No amount of cooperation can repay the loss incurred by compromise on such basic biblical truth. When evangelistic and church growth priorities are determined and maintained, cooperative efforts should not obstruct church growth. Cooperation, properly conceived and implemented can enhance growth but must be kept in proper bounds.

Spectacularism

Any detraction of emphasis on the place of local congregations in the redemptive plan of God restricts church growth. Spectacular, large-scale efforts, such as huge radio/TV ministries or extensive organizational entities can displace the position of the local church. Local churches sometimes suffer by comparison with highly professional television productions. In itself this situation is not destructive. I am not against the mass media approach so much as I am for the local expression of church life. The problem is that resources are often drained from local churches to large public approaches and the growth of the Christian movement restricted. It is sad when Christians replace local church life with the electronic church. Any time emphasis is directed away from local congregations to the sensational, mass expression of Christianity, *genuine church growth suffers.* Large-scale television or other mass media campaigns may bring attention to the participants but usually contributes little to balanced church growth.

The dangers of mass approaches can be minimized by keeping local congregations in a priority position. Resources channeled lavishly on mass media efforts can be at least partially rechanneled into local churches where more productive growth can be realized. Social ministry and efforts to achieve justice remain important aspects of Christian service. Local congregations must remain the center of Christian life and effort. The sensational, mass media approach should emphasize the place of the local church. Superchurches must seek to help, rather than live at the expense of small churches. Balanced church growth takes place primarily on the local level.

Persistence in the Unproductive

Persisting in the unproductive constitutes a major obstacle to growing churches. Churches and missionaries tend to settle into patterns of ministry. These patterns are sometimes unproductive—they do not lead to churches growing bigger, better, and broader. Remaining chained to the unproductive pattern, even when the pattern is obviously not leading to growth, obstructs church growth as few other problems.

Persistence sometimes grows out of a failure to recognize the possibilities of more productive patterns. A sense of hopelessness develops. With little or no vision for increased growth and little expectation of growth, a church or Mission may simply continue a "business as usual" approach and overlook growth possibilities.

At other times persistence in the unproductive stems from ideas that too much has been invested in a given pattern to even consider changing. This viewpoint is especially critical in regard to institutions. The investment of persons and money lead many to conclude that change is unwise if not impossible.

Consideration for feelings and protective attitudes keep many groups bound to the unproductive. Only spiritual giants can give of themselves in creating patterns of work and institutions of service and then be willing to set these patterns aside to seek more productive paths. It is difficult even to admit to ourselves and others that a pattern to which we have dedicated our lives is unproductive. Protectiveness thus leaves many tied to the less productive ways of work.

Conservatism in approach can be dictated by the sending body. The sending agencies often discourage, if not prohibit, creative alternatives. Resistance from the home base often cements a group to an unproductive or less productive pattern when more adequate strategies are available.

Persistence in the unproductive can be overcome. Changes can be made but only in response to dedication, persistence, and determination. Overcoming the problem of staying with the less productive demands attention to six steps.

Step one is recognizing and accepting the fact of unproductivity. Obviously, what is unproductive in one area may be productive in another due to differences of responsiveness. Every Mission, church, and missionary should use every means available to honestly and objectively assess the growth being realized as a result of the patterns employed.

Step two involves dedication to the concept of growth. Dedication to balanced church growth should be a higher priority than any other factor. No one wants to hurt feelings or be unkind. The fact is, however, that the growth of the Lord's Church is so imperative that nothing should be allowed to hinder it.

Step three is the formation of plans for change that give hope of increased results. Merely to point out unproductivity without plans for change effects little. Detailed plans with rationale are needed to reach the goal of change.

Sharing the facts and the plans for change is an imperative fourth step. Unilateral change on the part of the Mission, or the sponsoring church, or the missionaries (or a group of them) seldom brings about change without intense reaction. It is true that change may have to be put into operation before all involved fully agree with it. But every effort should be exerted to share the plans and the rationale with all concerned. Some delay in implementation can be tolerated in order to secure more agreement on and dedication to the change, but objection must not block necessary change.

Step five calls for implementing the needed change. This step demands courage and determination. It may at times be carried out in the face of opposition and lack of agreement. If the harvest is involved, the change must be made.

Finally, step six calls for analysis and evaluation of the new pattern. Simply changing strategy does not ensure growth. The new pattern should be as carefully evaluated as the old. If growth still lags, further change should be attempted.

Church growth is too important to allow any obstacle to impede progress. If unproductive patterns exist—or if previously productive ways no longer bear fruit—change must be introduced and productive patterns discovered. God has a way to balance growth and this way must be found and implemented.

Lost Contacts

Another obstacle to church growth related to the church itself is the loss of contact with the lost world, or what Donald McGavran has termed, "redemption and lift."[8] It is natural that the social condition of persons and groups who turn to Christianity will be upwardly mobile. Such social betterment is not only understandable it is to be expected. In itself, this mobility is not to be decried. The problem comes at the point of Christians and Christian groups becoming closed off and losing contact with thc nonChristian populations from which they came.

The solution to the problem of redemption and lift is certainly not found in any idea of bringing nominal, worldly persons into the church. On the other hand, the situation is little helped by promoting small, nongrowing enclaves of Christians among the multitudes of nonbelievers. The problem of lost contact with the unsaved world can be overcome if Christians and churches will follow these suggestions.

First, allow for and encourage those activities that will better the condition of the believers. The church should provide services that help people realize the possibilities for reaching higher plateaus of living. Care must be maintained that these lifting efforts not overshadow the evangelizing efforts of either Christians or churches.

A second step in rebuilding contact with the unsaved world is training the entire membership in the constant search for friendship and contact with the lost and uncommitted. Christians should be taught the validity of "making friends for Christ."[9] Any tendency for believers to prioritize Christian fellowship to the end that meaningful contact with the lost is sacrificed is a self-defeating strategy.

As a third help in guarding against the problem of lost contacts, the church can evangelize so as to maintain a stream of new converts coming into the fellowship. These new converts maintain many contacts (bridges) in the lost world. A new believer need not wait years until adequate training is given before being either encouraged or allowed to witness. Rather, the new believer may be the most effective evangelist as he or she shares the new experience in Christ.

The array of relationships in the lives of new converts provide ready-made contacts between the church and the world. Redemption and lift can be used positively when the lift is used to further the redemption of new converts. Redemption and lift, therefore, need not be obstacles to church growth. It only becomes an obstacle if meaningful contact with the unsaved world results. Effective evangelism, it will be remembered, demands, first of all, contact or presence.

Fellowship

Mutual love and fellowship among God's people enhance balanced church growth. Many things that are positive can, however, become obstructions to balanced growth. Fellowship, when it becomes an end in itself and cuts Christians off from the unchurched population, becomes pathological and destructive to the Church's mission. It then obstructs growth.

By fellowship we mean the network of interpersonal relationships that exists between believers, especially those believers who are members of a particular congregation. The mutual stimulation, support, comfort, and inspiration provide necessary aid in individual spiritual growth and in the growth of churches. Fellowship, rightly lived out, helps rather than hurts church growth.

Christian fellowship, sadly, can make reaching the unsaved and unchurched more difficult. The unity among members makes difficult the entrance of new persons into the fellowship. This problem can be particularly acute among youth groups. The growing church must be open in both membership and fellowship. Every church should be certain that the closeness of its Christian fellowship is open to including new people and making this openness clear to these new persons.

The answer to problems generated by the wrong emphasis on fellowship is simply to balance fellowship and penetration. Church members draw strength from the fellowship of saints but use this strength and inspiration to penetrate the world for witness and service. Christian fellowship should attract, not repell, the outsider. When correctly balanced, fellowship enhances the growth of both believers and churches.

Spiritual Obstacles

Of the barriers impacting the growth and ministry of churches, none are more serious than the spiritual obstacles. We will not discuss such matters as open sinfulness within the churches. Obviously, this condition lessens growth. Some of the spiritual obstacles to balanced church growth are defeatism, materialism, and nominalism.

Defeatism

One spiritual obstacle to church growth, defeatism, involves the lack of belief or faith that growth can or will take place. Defeatism often develops in regions where mission work faces long-term resistance to the gospel. Little growth easily becomes the norm, expectation decreases, and results tend to conform to these lowered expectations.

In time defeatism may turn to the exaltation of smallness. Small can be beautiful and the superchurch certainly does not constitute the ultimate goal of church growth. In some regions resistance dictates that churches will remain small. The Christian movement, however, must avoid the defeatism that accepts little growth as the norm and remains satisfied with little growth when the harvest remains ungathered.

Overcoming defeatism demands a renewed belief that God desires growth and the Holy Spirit provides power for harvest. Discouragement stems from considering the waves; victory comes through contemplating the Christ who can still the storm. Accepting God's assurance of power helps dispell defeatism (Matt. 28:18). New vision can often cure defeatism.

Correctly assessing the situation may likewise relieve defeatist feelings. Lack of harvest or slow growth may spring from faulty methods or wrong emphasis rather than lack of response. Changing methods often is the solution to defeatism. Missionaries can continue to accept little growth from one segment of a population while overlooking nearby groups who are open to evangelization. Defeatism must never be allowed to blind God's messengers to the waiting harvest.

Defeatism can be overcome by commitment to growth. Growth in numbers saved and churches planted remains the first priority. When situations make such growth slower, concentration on other aspects of growth remains possible. The important principle remains—God's people must be committed to and constantly seek balanced growth in his churches.

Materialism

A devastating spiritual obstacle to balanced church growth, materialism, refers simply to any self-centered, self-serving, self-seeking tendency in churches, denominations, or church leaders. The spirit of materialism is evident when a local church delays mission activity for the sake of providing equipment, facilities, or additional staff. Materialism becomes a factor when motivation springs from desire to build a personal empire or attract attention to self. Materialism has become the problem when churches or denominations are more concerned with advancing their own group than with the progress of God's kingdom. Materialism obstructs church growth anytime God's churches and God's people become self-centered and seek personal or corporate advance at the expense of servant activity.

Balanced church growth is impossible in the face of self-seeking materialism in churches or church leaders. The attitude of materialism drives churches to leave needy places of ministry to seek the easier fields. Materialism and self-seeking leads to inauthentic evangelism and church growth as churches and leaders major on the spectacular rather than on service. Materialism causes churches and leaders to demand to be served rather than seek to give self on behalf of others.

The only cure for materialism is repentance. Repentance carries the idea of leaving the old, self-seeking pattern and turning to the new, servant pattern. Materialism, a manifestation of sinfulness in the church, severely restricts balanced church growth. The concluding chapter of this book considers the only cure to this obstacle—the adoption of the servant pattern.

Nominalism

Nominalism, the listless attitude of routine faith and church life, obstructs church growth. Nominalism not only results in limited efforts toward outreach but also the lukewarm church attracts few people. Thus, nominalism hinders church growth from two directions.

C. Peter Wagner calls nominalism "St. John's Syndrome." He writes:

> The underlying problem of St. John's Syndrome is Christian nominality. When

> Christians become Christians in name only, when they feel that their faith is only routine, when church involvement is largely going through the motions, and when belonging to church is a family tradition and a social nicety, St. John's Syndrome is likely at work.[10]

Wagner continues by identifying St. John's Syndrome with the "institutional stage" of a church's development. While it may be true that nominalism most often sets in during later stages of a church's development, such is not always the case. The tragedy of nominalism threatens churches and their growth at every stage of life.

The causes and results of nominalism are obvious in the accounts of the churches at Ephesus (Rev. 2:1-7) and Laodicea (Rev. 3:14-22). Nominalism had invaded the Ephesian church because it had left its first love (Rev. 2:4). This church demonstrated internal stability and growth. It stood against persecution and adversity (perseverance). It remained doctrinally correct (tested false apostles). It remained morally pure (cannot endure evil men). It remained nominal because it had left the first love of commitment to evangelism. What were the deeds that this church had done at first that it was no longer doing (Rev. 2:5)? I believe that Paul's letter to the Ephesians was a circular written to many congregations in the region of Ephesus. Could this not indicate that the early Ephesian church was active in starting many congregations? Is it not possible that the Ephesian church to which John referred had moved away from church multiplication and therefore grown nominal? I cannot prove this but it is a decided possibility.

How was the nominalism (whatever its source) to be overcome. The apostle John simply instructed the church to remember, repent, and return (Rev. 2:5). Churches today that have allowed nominalism to obstruct growth must remember the days of growth and commitment, repent of the failures, turn away from the unproductive, and return to the first love which I believe is evangelism and church planting.

Nominalism at Laodicea sprang from a different source (Rev. 3:14-22). Lukewarmness seems to have resulted from self-satisfaction and the failure to perceive spiritual needs (Rev. 3:17-18). The Laodicean church relied on its wealth, its knowledge of medicine, its sufficiency, rather than the Lord. Self-sufficiency naturally leads to nominalism. The cure of nominalism in the case of Laodicea was the recognition of need, the acceptance of God's power and strength, and the realization of God's loving discipline (Rev. 3:18-20).

Nominalism remains an enemy of balanced church growth. Churches and denominations easily fall victims to nominalism, growth declines, leading to still further nominalism. Christians stop growing spiritually, soul-winning is neglected, nominalism increases, spiritual progress further declines. Nominalism is overcome by continued commitment to spiritual growth and evangelistic outreach. Neglecting either growth or outreach leads to trouble. Keeping both in balance defeats nominalism and allows growth to continue.

Conclusion

There are obstacles to balanced church growth. Some obstacles are simply manifestations of sin in the camp. Other obstacles are evidences of confused methods and priorities. Still others stem from misunderstanding. The important fact is that no obstacle is insurmountable and none need be permanent. Ways to avoid and overcome obstacles are available. To maintain balanced church growth demands God's people be alert to their dangers, quick to acknowledge their presence, and dedicated to their destruction within the body.

Further Reading

C. Peter Wagner, *Your Church Can Be Healthy* (Regal)
Lyle E. Schaller, *Hey, That's Our Church* (Abingdon)
Douglas Alan Walrath, *Leading Churches Through Change* (Abingdon)
Howard A. Snyder, *The Problem of Wineskins* (IVP)
Lyle E. Schaller, *Assimilating New Members* (Abingdon)

Notes

1. Harold Lindsell, "Missionary Imperatives: A Conservative Evangelical Exposition," in *Protestant Cross-currents in Mission*, ed. Norman H. Horner (Nashville: Abingdon Press, 1968), pp. 58-59.
2. Alan R. Tippett, *Verdict Theology in Missionary Theory*, p. 91.
3. Donald A. McGavran, *How Churches Grow*, p. 105.
4. Ibid., p. 98.
5. C. Peter Wagner, *Frontiers in Missionary Strategy*, p. 170.
6. C. Peter Wagner, *Your Church Can Be Healthy* (Glendale, Calif.: Regal Books, 1979), pp. 64-76.

7. Lyle Schaller, "Reflections on Cooperative Missions," *The Clergy Journal* (September 1977):21.

8. Donald A. McGavran, *Understanding Church Growth,* pp. 295-313.

9. See Wayne McDill, *Making Friends for Christ* (Nashville: Broadman Press, 1980) and Win and Charles Arn, *Making Disciples God's Way* (Pasadena: Church Growth Press, 1982).

10. Wagner, *Your Church Can Be Healthy,* p. 112.

7
Finding Keys to Church Planting

Church planting holds a prominent place in Church Growth thinking. Beginning responsible churches that reproduce themselves, far from denominational empire-building, is a primary method of working with the Holy Spirit to evangelize the peoples of the world. The necessity of and strategies for the unlimited multiplication of churches has already been discussed.

Four kinds of church growth have been identified and named. Internal growth relates to the church's own progress and the progress of its members. This growth in grace and Christlikeness, while imperative, must never be allowed exclusive place in the church's life. In the growth of a church, as in other aspects of Christian living, one who concentrates exclusively on self ends up losing all. Charles Chaney says that a church can strangle on a totally inward focus.[1]

Expansion growth relates to the church's imperative task of evangelizing and incorporating people from its own community. Through expansion growth the church reaches its own kinds of people. This kind of growth composes the primary thrust of most churches. Important as expansion growth is, it is not the only kind of growth.

Extension growth, one of the quickest ways to start new churches, provides for the planting of a daughter church among basically the same types of people as the mother church. Churches should be on the lookout for opportunities to plant new churches among like populations of people. A church can give several families to be seed families in the new congregation. In this way the church grows by extension.

Bridging growth takes place when a church plants a new congregation in a different cultural, linguistic, or racial community. If the cultural barrier crossed is relatively small—for example a middle-class Anglo church starting a congregation for a lower socio-economic group—it is called bridging one. If, however, the cultural barrier is larger, for example for a different ethnic or language group, the growth could be called bridging two. The Anglo church that plants a congregation for an Asian community, using the Asian language, would be achieving bridging two growth.

Church planting relates to both extension and bridging growth. New congregations are essential to the effort to win the world to Jesus. This chapter, therefore, presents methods and strategies for starting new churches by both extension and bridging growth.

Persuading

Not every church person is convinced of the need for new congregations. "We already have enough churches," is an excuse often given by both churches and individuals who lack commitment to new congregations. Resistance to new churches may be encountered among lay workers, pastors of area churches, missionaries, denominational workers, and leaders of other denominations. A first step in church planting often lies in the area of persuading—sharing the need and demand for extension and bridging growth. Until men and women are convinced of the need for a new congregation, little growth will occur. In the words of Charles Brock: "In the power of the Holy Spirit, Bible believers have no other alternative than to scale the barriers, narrow the limitations, and move in step with God in pushing back the frontiers of paganism, by the rapid establishment of indigenous churches."[2]

Both Jack Redford and Charles Chaney use the term "creating a climate for church planting" in their discussions of the persuading process.[3] To create a climate for church planting, churches and missions must be prepared spiritually, mentally, organizationally, and purposefully.

Church planting is a spiritual undertaking and must begin with spiritual preparation. Biblical admonitions toward evangelism and church planting provide a solid foundation for church multiplication. The central place of the Holy Spirit both in the life of a church and the lives and service of church members must be stressed in a congregation.

Charles Chaney, in an adaptation of ideas from Melvin Hodges, suggests four truths about the Holy Spirit and church planting that relate to the adequate spiritual preparation of a church on mission. Chaney admonishes:

> The necessity for all believers to be filled with and to walk in the Spirit . . . the need for all Christians to be led by the Spirit in their daily lives and to surrender themselves to God as instruments of righteousness, and then to become productive members of the body of Christ . . . the responsibility of each

> believer to attempt to discover the particular gift given him or her by the Spirit, and to exercise this gift so that the church might be built up and continue to grow . . . that the Holy Spirit empowers the most backward Christian for effective ministry and witness.[4]

Spiritual preparation is not "a step" in church planting. This effort to maintain spiritual undergirding for the work must remain an ongoing process of the group. Periodic renewal and recommitment is imperative. Planting churches must never be reduced to a mechanically achieved duty. Church planting should be seen as the spiritual undertaking of converted Christians working through the Holy Spirit and the gifts he grants to reach the biblical goal of winning men and women to Christ and incorporating them into responsible, reproducing congregations.

The group (church or mission) also needs mental preparation. Understanding the need for church planting provides an indispensable foundation for effective ministry. Opportunities and needs of church planting must be clearly in the minds of leaders and members. Commitment to church planting flourishes following understanding of the need for and methods of starting new congregations. The local church must see beyond its own needs. Information alone will never prepare a church, a denomination, or a mission for church planting—but information concerning unreached peoples and areas is a starting point in the persuading process.

There must be organizational preparation. Every denomination, mission, and local church needs a dedicated group charged with the responsibility of leading the group in church planting activity. Jack Redford calls this group the Church Missions Committee[5] and Charles Chaney names it a Church Planting Task Force.[6] Mission groups ordinarily have a committee that leads the group in plans for new work. By whatever name, this committee or task force is given the responsibility of leading the church planting efforts.

Perhaps Chaney's designation is better. A Church Missions Committee or a Mission Outreach Committee can become bogged down in many "mission" activities. Most, if not all, of the "mission" activities are valid, needed, and proper. Starting new churches can, however, be easily lost or put off in face of the many other mission tasks. The church mission committee can be given such a variety of responsibilities that real planning for opening new areas or starting new churches is neglected. There should be some group dedicated exclusively to leadership in church planting.

This task force or planning committee needs ongoing training. Initial training can be achieved through written materials and teaching sessions. Eventually, the training will be in the field as the committee members actually participate in church planting efforts.

Chaney suggests five primary functions of the Church Planting Task Force (hereafter referred to as CPT).[7] The prophetic function involves inspiring and motivating the church or mission about new work and keeping the fires burning. The committee or task force serves, as Chaney predicts, as the mission conscience of the church. The mission planning committee should keep the idea of new areas and new work before the eyes of the missionaries, national leaders, or the Church.

The CPT also fulfills the planning function. Thorough study of the area and its needs helps the CPT to discover the needs for new churches. Studies of the areas surveyed by mission groups should be filed for future reference. This study and planning function should be ongoing. Plans for continuing outreach must be a part of the work of the CPT. The mission planning committee has a special responsibility to provide detailed studies of areas under consideration for new work.

The CPT likewise provides a promotive function. By sharing the needs and plans for new work, the CPT guides the thinking and dedication of the entire group toward commitment to new churches. Church planting is the business of the entire group—not just a dedicated few. Until the fervor for new work permeates the entire church or mission, church planting will not take its rightful place in the ministry.

The performing function of the CPT follows the prophetic, planning, and promoting functions. Performance here takes the meaning of getting the job done. The CPT enlists and trains people to involve themselves in the new work. The CPT continues oversight and direction as the new work begins. Constant evaluation is maintained. New plans are allowed to grow out of existing efforts.

Experience in church planting indicates that failures and difficulties often can be traced to a lack of planning and commitment on the part of sponsoring churches, pastors, missions, and other entities. Sponsoring a new church in name only seldom produces desired outcomes. Paying lip service to new work when the real goal is building up the existing church or churches frustrates church planting efforts.

Creating a climate for church planting involves preparing the churches and missions in commitment (Chaney speaks of this as the fifth function of the CPT, preparing the church pragmatically). The church or mission must commit itself in terms of people, money, training, and effort. Without this commitment, church planting will be lost.

Of these areas in which commitment is necessary, the most vital may be the area of people. Churches are often more willing to give money than involve people in missions. Short-term involvement in missions (mission trips, weekend involvements, etc.) are growing in popularity. While these mission activities bring wholesome rewards, they must never be allowed to substitute for long-term involvement. Churches can contribute some of their people as seed families to new work. Leaders should be commissioned to help begin new work. It is safe to say that no church ever really loses by giving of its members to begin a new church.

Missions must guard against the tendency to employ the bulk of resources —both financial and people—in existing programs. Missionary institutions have an insatiable appetite for missionary personnel. There seems to be a willingness to staff institutions at the expense of new work. Seldom is an institutional worker redeployed to new work. In most mission endeavors, the entire body of workers can be readily absorbed in existing efforts. The mission (denomination) must guard against the tendency to consume resources in existing work with the result of having no resources for new churches.

Church planting relies heavily on a sponsoring entity—a church or a Mission. This reliance on the sponsoring group demands adequate preparation. Church planting requires a particular climate—providing this climate is an exciting beginning for the task of starting new churches. Persuading people, churches, or missions sometimes is the most demanding task of all.

Preparing

Once the sponsoring church or Mission is persuaded as to the need for new work, actual preparation for the effort begins. Many efforts at new work fail because of a failure to plan. Inadequate planning makes successful church planting unlikely.

Decide on a Goal

Planning for a new church demands a clear insight as to the goal for the new congregation. The goal will include not only the creation of a new congregation but the planting of a particular kind of congregation. Care must be taken that the type of church planted will meet the needs of the community.

It is necessary to consider the kind of church that is to come into existence. A church for a language or ethnic group will require special plans. A church that will meet in a house requires different planning than one that plans to become a superchurch. A neighborhood church needs different planning than a regional church. Obviously, the community and group to be served influences the type of church that will be planted. An imperative step remains deciding on the goal. Once this decision is made, planning can proceed.

Select Areas For New Churches

A denomination should have a church extension division or department. A Mission needs a new work committee. A local church functions through a church missions committee or church planting task force. One or more than one of these groups in concert will lead in selecting areas for new work.

Several books on church planting give detailed lists of criteria for choosing an area for new work.[8] In this more general approach, we will sum up their criteria and suggest some methods that can be used to discover where new churches should be placed.

Criterion one: The possibility of a church in the area is favorable. Remember, response rather than need determines the use of resources. Masses of people naturally attract the evangelist. It is not, however, the mere presence of numbers of people but presence of people who show signs of response that guide in the selection of an area. Is there indication that response will come and a church can be maintained?

Criterion two: The need for a church and its ministry is apparent. Certainly, the ratio of unchurched people relates to the need for a new church. The needs for church ministry likewise relate to this selection process. A combination of unmet needs for salvation and church membership along with opportunities for social ministries sets a strong demand for new work. Can a church provide a needed ministry in the area?

Criterion three: Groups that need a church who are not being evangelized are present. A community may have several churches but still not have congregations targeted for every ethnic, racial, or socio-economic group in the area. When unchurched pockets of people are present, the need for new churches is established. Are there groups who are not being reached by existing churches?

Criterion four: Evangelistic witness and church activity are inadequate. The mere presence of church buildings and even congregations does not ensure adequate evangelical witness and service. New churches should be placed where the evangelistic witness and social service is inadequate. Are there ministry needs not fulfilled?

Criterion five: Regional needs indicate the need for and possibilities of new churches. In selecting an area for new work, attention must be given to entire regions not simply isolated areas. Charles Chaney describes need for and methods of a regional plan for congregationalizing a broad area.[9] Regional planning must avoid the road-map syndrome. The fact that a large city where we have no church is located between two cities in which we have work does not automatically indicate that city as the prime location for new work. Romantic notions of having churches on both sides of the river do not indicate the places for new work. The notoriety of an area does not automatically stamp it as the place for new work. Regional planning should be both scientific and Spirit-led to find the areas most suitable for church planting.

These, and other criteria guide as areas for new work are selected. The criteria for areas needing new churches are not always obvious. There are, however, methods that can direct a denomination, a Mission, or a church to indicators that show where new churches are needed. The following methods help discover the most promising areas for new churches.

The most obvious of these indicators, a direct approach, considers geographical factors that call for new churches. A request from a group living in an area often forces attention on the area and its need. Churches and Missions should be ready to respond to direct requests for new churches. Care must be exercised, however. A direct request, by itself, does not assure that a new congregation should be planted. Even when direct requests are received, the church or Mission should carefully consider to see that the criteria for a new church are met.

In many cases the Church (church) will use the investigative approach to ascertain the need for new churches. These investigations include detailed studies of communities—population, groups of persons, church membership facts, community needs, and challenges to church ministry. J. V. Thomas calls this kind of investigation a feasibility study.[10]

Feasibility type studies make use of the voluminous data of the census reports, information from city planning offices and a drive-through, visual observation of the community. The feasibility study makes extensive use of a door-to-door sampling of the community. Results of this sampling should be carefully considered and preserved.

Information from the detailed study of the area reveals the number of unchurched persons, groups of unchurched persons, needs in the community and possibilities for church ministry. On the basis of this data, and through the leading of the Holy Spirit, areas for and the types of new works can be ascertained.

In overseas missions and in many new areas of work in the United States, the need for new churches in almost every area will be obvious. In such cases, it must be remembered that response rather than need should determine the allocation of resources. The question is not simply, "Is a church needed?" but also, "Are the possibilities for a church good?" New churches should be first planted in areas where they have the likelihood of surviving. To minister to an area, a church must *continue to exist.*

Finding the area for new work may also follow the realization approach. This approach emerges when an obvious need arises. New developments often lead to such realization of opportunity for new work. When a new city such as Brazilia, Brazil, or The Woodlands, Texas, comes into existence, the need for new churches cannot be denied. Church bodies must remain on the alert for such developments and have long-range plans for meeting their needs.

Sites for Church Buildings

In church planting, places for church buildings must be considered. When decisions to secure a site are delayed, space often proves unavailable or too expensive. Buying strategic land for future church sites pays great dividends in church planting. It allows for space that otherwise might be unavailable.

The purchase of a church site does not, however, prescribe that the church must be located on the site. Developments might indicate another site to be better. In such cases the church planters should be willing to change locations, even in face of some financial loss. Do not locate the church on an inadequate site just because that land has already been purchased. The future of the church is more important than financial considerations.

Once preparation has been made, the next step relates to implementing the plans. This step might be called the producing stage. Again, we would remember that the Holy Spirit must infuse all—persuading, planning, and producing.

Producing

The actual process by which the church is planted follows lines of contact, meeting, establishing, growing, and reproducing.

Contact

Jack Redford correctly notes that churches can jump too quickly into the phase of public meetings. There should be a time of cultivation in the community before starting services. Again, Redford says, "Apart from selecting the right community in which to plant a new church, perhaps the single most important element in a right beginning is community cultivation."[11] Cultivation of the area for new work includes contact in the sense of meeting people in the community and becoming known. Community relations should be carefully built. Contact with existing churches, mission groups, with government and community bodies, with businesses in the area, and with the population in general provides a good foundation for the new church's work.

The group planning to begin the new church should seek opportunity at community ministry through which love and concern can be demonstrated. This demonstration can help pave the way for the church. Relating to community activities and needs provides valid contact with the community.

It is not impossible that this contact with the community—especially the religious sector—will result in discouraging statements and opposition. A community and its religious leaders may seek to dissuade the beginning of a new church. These leaders may even erect barriers to the new work. Sometimes property owners do not want a church building located in their neighborhood. Careful consideration must be given to these objections but the Lord's will must claim our loyalty.

Meeting

The next stage of church planting relates to meeting. Persons are visited and enlisted for some type of fellowship meeting. Various styles of meeting can be used—Bible study, worship services, revival, a Christian forum which discusses topics of interest, and fellowship meetings. In church planting, Bible study or Bible reading groups have proved most useful. In fact, whatever style might be used, the Bible should be central.

The purpose of the mission fellowship or the Bible study/reading group is to lead new persons to salvation, reclaim strayed believers, and incorporate Christians into the new Christian fellowship. This fellowship should continue until the group has the strength to proceed to the stage of establishing the new church.

Establishing

The new congregation must achieve recognition as a church in the eyes of the members themselves, in the minds of the community, and in the thoughts of the sponsoring group—be that a church, a Mission, a denomination, or other entity. In the establishing stage the new church will care for those matters of organization (bylaws, etc.), provide facilities, equipment, and the formal constitution of the group. The methods of effecting these acts may vary. To ensure proper relationship and secure more support for the new church, the accepted methods of establishing the new church should be followed, according to the Mission, denomination, government, or culture.

Sooner or later the need to provide facilities will arise. Finding an adequate site, forming a master building plan, and accomplishing the building effort could easily consume all the time and effort of the new church. Care must be exercised that the provision of facilities does not detract from the more important task of winning and building people. The period of providing facilities is both a critical and dangerous time for the new church. Church buildings are often necessary. It is well, however, to keep the building program as only one element in the process of establishing the church.

Growing

New churches should be planted with the idea of growing. It is important that the establishing of the church *not* be seen as the final accomplishment. Church growth, it will be remembered, concerns churches growing bigger, better, and broader. The denomination, mission, or church that plants a church will be concerned that the new church can and will grow in both numbers and quality. The purpose of church growth is planting churches that continue to grow, serve, and reproduce.

Reproducing

Charles Brock is exactly right in saying that church planting should "think reproducible." He says, "A church planter cannot be sure every church he plants will actually begin new churches, but he can do everything possible to leave the way open for such a self-reproducing church."[12] From the first, reproduction should be built into the mind-set and the plans of the new church.

Many churches become inverted and see only their own needs and plans. The new church should receive a strong missionary spirit and dedication. Again, the goal is responsible, reproducing believers in responsible, reproducing congregations.

Conclusion

Church planting must remain a central interest and activity of Church Growth Theory. The only way to meet the needs of the fantastically growing populations of the world is by providing fantastically multiplying churches.[13] Almost every community needs more churches. Missions and churches today must emphasize a vast church planting if they are to remain faithful to the Lord of the harvest. The commission—make disciples—demands the provision of churches into which these disciples can be incorporated and developed.

Questions and Activities

1. Secure and show the film, "Planned Parenthood for Churches" from the Home Mission Board, SBC.
2. Make a survey (feasibility study) to find an area where a new church is needed. Contact persons or groups that could help start a church in the area.
3. Why do some people resist the idea of new churches?
4. Find the population of your community and the number of churches in your community. Are there sufficient churches? Are all groups of people cared for?

Further Reading

David J. Hesselgrave, *Planting Churches Cross Culturally* (Baker)
Charles Brock, *The Principles and Practice of Indigenous Church Planting* (Broadman)
Jack Redford, *Planting New Churches* (Broadman)

Charles L. Chaney, *Church Planting at the End of the Twentieth Century* (Tyndale)
Timothy Starr, *Church Planting: Always in Season* (Fellowship of Evangelical Baptist Churches in Canada)

Notes

1. Charles Chaney, *Church Planting at the End of the Twentieth Century* (Wheaton, Ill.: Tyndale House Publishers, Inc., 1982), pp. 84-85.
2. Charles Brock, *The Principles and Practice of Indigenous Church Planting* (Nashville: Broadman Press, 1981), p. 96.
3. Jack Redford, *Planting New Churches* (Nashville: Broadman Press, 1978), pp. 17-18; Chaney, pp. 77 ff.
4. Chaney, p. 82.
5. Redford, pp. 28-33.
6. Chaney, pp. 86-89.
7. Ibid., pp. 88-89.
8. Redford, pp. 34-45; Chaney, pp. 39-58.
9. Chaney, pp. 39-59.
10. J. V. Thomas, "Feasibility Study," Baptist General Convention of Texas.
11. Redford, pp. 52-60.
12. Brock, p. 56.
13. McGavran, "Wrong Strategy: The Real Crisis in Missions," p. 3.

8
Developing Urban Church Growth Patterns

The world increasingly becomes an urban place. As cities expand population-wise and space-wise, they also expand in significance for modern mankind. Little wonder that Donald A. McGavran writes:

> Discipling urban populations is perhaps the most urgent task confronting the Church. Bright hope gleams that now is precisely the time to learn how it may be done and to surge forward actually doing it.[1]

Roger Greenway correctly notes that the "pith helmet" approach to missions, that centered on rural peoples and tribal groups, no longer fits the situation.[2] The realities of urban life must be faced—its needs assessed, its differences accepted, its possibilities seized. Balanced church growth must invade the urban world and develop patterns for reaching urban peoples.

The charge that church growth has nothing for the cities is as unjustified as it is unfounded.[3] It is true that much Church Growth Theory has been developed and implemented among tribal, rural peoples of the less developed nations. The basic approaches and strategies of Church Growth are, however, not only adaptable to urban life but also hold the major hope for effective urban evangelism. We must develop patterns for urban church ministry.

The Strategic Importance of Cities

Between 1980 and 2000 church growth will take place increasingly, though not exclusively, in the strategic urban spaces. The importance of cities must not blind Christian missions to the vast possibilities and needs of nonurbanites. If by AD 2000, 55 percent of the world's expected 6.3 billion people live in cities,[4] 2.8 billion rural people will remain to be reached. Still, church growth must look to the staggering populations, the concentrated political-economic power, the frightening problems, and perceive the unlimited possibilities for church ministry that exist in urban areas.

Population Factors

Worldwide increase of urbanization with its consequent compacting of urban peoples seizes the attention of urban church planners. Almost onehalf the world's people (41 percent) lived in cities in 1980. In the More Developed Countries (hereafter referred to as MDCs) over seven of ten persons (72 percent) were urbanites. In the Less Developed Countries (hereafter referred to as LDCs) one of three lived in cities.[5] While in the United States three of four persons live in urban areas, some nations report even higher rates of urbanization. For example, Sweden, West Germany, Denmark, Netherlands, Australia, New Zealand, Chile, Venezuela, Uraguay, and Argentina were 80 percent urban in 1980. At the same time Singapore, Hong King, and Kuwait show an urban population in excess of 90 percent.[7]

The sheer numbers of persons represented by urban population figures, while impressive, do not exhaust the significance of urbanization for church growth thinking. Urban populations are as heterogeneous as they are compacted. The diverse groupings of peoples in the urban environment pose a distinctive challenge for churches and denominations. Churches composed of essentially middle-class, Anglo members, which hold middle-class ways and values, find it difficult, if not impossible, to attract the poor, the ethnic, the outcasts of the cities. Clearly, both the numbers and the diverse nature of urban populations contribute to the necessity of patterns and strategies for urban church growth.

Political-Economic Factors

Population migrates to the cities. Political and economic power increasingly reside in these same urban spaces. Industrialism provided the impetus for urbanization. Political and economic power was tied to the manufacturing centers. In postindustrial society, with heavy emphasis on information-intensive, service-provision, leisure-central factors, cities will become even more the possessors of political and economic prestige.

Replacement, in many cities, of machine politics by reformed government patterns which stress councils and managers, has in no wise lessened the political or economic clout of cities. National elections are won or lost in the cities. Economic policies are made mainly for the cities and the lion's share of resources are expended to meet city needs.

This political and economic significance of the world must be addressed by churches and church growth thinkers alike. Religious groups have abdicated responsibility for and thereby lost influence in governmental and economic sectors. Biblical principles demand that churches and Christians exert positive influence on the political and economic institutions that reside in the city. Only viable, visible, influential churches and church leaders can recapture the proper and significant place of churches in urban politics and economics.

Problems and Possibilities in Urban Environments

The magnitude of both problems and possibilities in urban areas underlines the significance of urban church ministry. Johannes F. Linn traces urban problems, especially in developing countries, to two primary phenomena. He says that urban labor supply tends to expand more rapidly than urban labor demand. This limits the growth of urban wages and incomes, especially for the unskilled. Secondly, according to Linn, the demand for urban services expands more rapidly than supply leading to rising prices for urban land and housing, overcrowding, and shortages of public services. The resulting imbalances are largely due to the inefficiency of government policy. Thus, Linn traces the problems of city life to mismanagement.[8]

Every city has a unique set of problems that sounds remarkably like the unique problems of every other city. Typical city problems relate to overcrowding, shortages of essential services, expanding slum areas, increasing congestion, unemployment and underemployment, racial and minority unrest and tension, environmental decline, crime, and issues of land usage. These and other problems lead to administrative demands such as planning, financial provision, and the maintenance of order.

Many, if not most, of these problems seen in MDCs are not only present but intensified in LDCs. Something of the financial difficulties of cities in LDCs can be seen in the fact that in many LDC cities, it would demand one-third of the annual income of a poor family simply to provide a sanitation facility.[9] These problems of housing, employment, sanitation, crowding, and crime, while accentuated in many LDC cities, are certainly far from inconsequential in MDCs.

Added to and compounded by the "macro" problems of cities, urban churches must face and attempt to aleviate the "micro," or personal problems of many urbanites. Disillusionment, loss of community, anomie, rebellion, and anger lead to moral decline with its consequent narcotic and alcohol abuse as well as family disintegration. Paul Geisel rightly says, "Our cities are short on justice, tranquillity, and general welfare."[10] Churches must deal with the multitudes of personal tragedies in the cities.

Urban church growth patterns must conceive of these urban problems as possibilities rather than obstacles. Church groups have allowed urban problems to overwhelm and consequently have surrendered the cities, and city services, to secular institutions. Urban church ministry must see urban problems as opportunities for service and that service as an evangelistic opportunity. Patterns for urban church ministry must interface with urban problems. As urban churches communicate the gospel through word and deed, service opens doors of redemptive power to city dwellers.

I do not minimize urban problems or the difficulties they pose for city churches. I do believe that churches have allowed the problems in the cities to overshadow the tremendous possibilities these problems provide. These possibilities for both witness and service must have priority in urban ministry patterns.

Cities, due to the magnitude of their populations, the centrality of their political and economic power, the complexity of their problems, and the vastness of their possibilities hold a place of significance for church growth. The great mission fields of the world's cities must receive proper and immediate attention as urban patterns are discovered and developed.

Churches and the Cities

Traditional church response to cities has been retreat. Church buildings often have been located in city areas which increasingly felt the impact of change. As immigrant groups and the rural poor packed into the cities, the middle-class membership of these traditional churches fled to the suburbs. Churches found themselves both more compatible with and attracted to the affluent suburbanites than to the inner-city poor. Racial and linguistic barriers often added to the alienation felt by both the churches and the newcomers. The churches have been left with neither the desire nor the skill to minister to the people living in their area.

Typically churches responded to the changing situation either by leaving the area occupied by these different peoples and joining the flight to the suburbs, or by remaining at the original church site with members returning from the suburbs for worship and other church activities. The isolation of the second response often proved more detrimental than the absence of the church in the first response.

In either case meaningful contact with the peoples in the city was lost and church influence minimized. The error is not so much in the church following its own as they migrate. Indeed, following your own is an acceptable Church Growth Strategy. The error lies in neglecting the newer people in the old area of work. The vacuum left by a retreating church, whether the retreat came by physical departure or psychological isolation, most often goes unfilled. The result is large segments of unevangelized people.

The situation we are describing often happens in communities experiencing the entrance of peoples of lower socio-economic status. These poorer, less educated, groups are often not served by the churches they formerly attended. Consequently, the urban poor remain largely isolated from churches and from the gospel. The urban poor may, in fact, constitute the greatest mission field in the United States today. In LDNs the vast numbers of urban poor are even less evangelized and therefore more in need of the Church than the poor in the MDNs. Viable, congruent, evangelistic, ministering churches are needed in today's cities.

Too many churches have become middle-class enclaves, cut off from the lower classes. The isolation stems as much from the lower classes as from the middle-class church members. This is to say that the middle-class churches are sometimes more open to the lower class people than the lower classes are open to attending the middle-class churches. To overcome this problem churches must commit themselves to the cities and city people and seek to break down barriers to their evangelization.

Churches and denominations must become acclimated to and comfortable in the cities. New ways must be devised and implemented. Larry Rose and Kirk Hadaway catch this spirit, saying:

> Our cities will not be good places to live in if churches and their influence are not presented in an effective way to the people in the cities. It is, therefore, our mandate not to stand on the sidelines and criticize but to become a real catalyst in the cities, to change them, to raise their values and their sense of caring. The challenge of urbanization for churches in the 1980s can be what the challenge of the illegal religion status was to early churches in the first century; for, in spite of the difficulties and adversities, churches grew and expanded their witness into the world.[11]

Components of an Urban Ministry Model

Many cries are raised on behalf of urban ministry. In these cries, disparaging words outnumber optimistic statements. There is, however, agreement as to the need of an urban strategy. Any attempt to formulate strategies for urban ministry must include at least seven components. These components can be mixed and adapted according to the specific needs of particular situations but all must be present in viable urban strategy.

A first and primary component in an urban model is commitment. The retreat from the city, too often seen in urban church approach, reveals a lack of commitment to urban ministry. Aversion rather than attraction characterizes the religious approach to the urban scene. Commitment to the city involves loving determination to meet the needs of city dwellers rather than simply seek the advancement of a particular congregation in the more easily reached suburbs.

Commitment to urban ministry demands commitment to change. Cities are changing. Urban populations are changing. The church (or Church) that attempts to maintain traditional and long-standing patterns of ministry and/or membership will eventually lose capacity for urban service. Change, while often traumatic, is necessary for effective urban ministry.

Commitment to balanced church growth in cities involves first the decision to stay and to change so as to reach and serve urbanites. No strategy can be effective in the city without this pavement-level commitment. Only as urban strategy is based on this commitment can urban ministry become a reality.

A second component of a viable urban pattern, optimism relates to the ability to see potential, to dream, to expect. The vision for growth spoken of in chapter 1 is of particular significance for urban ministry. The conviction that cities can be reached for Christ and that city dwellers hold tremendous possibilities for the churches is essential for sound urban planning and effort.

G. Willis Bennett is obviously correct in saying that churches must be willing to set goals and implement new plans of action in the urban areas. Such implementation may, he says, "require the church to dream some new dreams." Bennett continues that the church that does not dream new dreams and thus implement new plans "runs the risk of losing its effectiveness."[12]

Optimism, rather than defeatism, must be incorporated into all urban strategies. Urban church growth awaits workers with positive attitudes toward the city and its people. For too long the Church has tended to see the city as an evil place. Optimism undergirds effective urban strategy.

A third component of urban strategy is urban eyes, that is, a basic understanding of and empathy with cities, urban problems, and city dwellers. The Christian movement needs a corps of professionally trained urbanologists who understand cities and their problems. These urban specialists, trained in both urban affairs and urban church ministry, can help forge the plans for reaching city populations. Since traditional approaches are not reaching the cities, new approaches must be formulated and such new approaches need the insights and understandings of urban specialists.

Urban patterns must contain, as a fourth component, provision for the plurality that exists and thrives in the cities of the world. While highly visible in cities in the United States, this pluralism is even more apparent and significant for church growth in many third world cities. Urban strategy must make provision for each of the varying groups who are packed into urban spaces.

In order to meet the needs of the city's plurality, urban strategy must include plans for reaching and serving every segment of the mosaic that comprises urban society. Should existing churches be unable (or unwilling) to meet the specific needs of new kinds of people entering the area, then new churches designed to evangelize and minister to these segments of the population should be planted and cultivated.

In urban spaces there should be congregations designed to attract and minister to the poor, the rich, and the middle classes. There should be churches targeted toward the professionals, the blue-collar workers, and the underemployed. There should be congregations for various ethnic and language groups. Plurality is a fact of urban life and must, therefore, be a factor in urban church strategy.

Urban strategy will not be content with providing for the various segments of urban society. The next factor in urban society calls for bridging between peoples to further both evangelism and brotherhood between groups. Caring for plurality in the city includes bringing differing groups of believers into the unity in Christ that can come only through the power of the cross and the work of the Spirit.

A fifth component of urban strategy calls for proper balance between evangelism and social involvement. Evangelism must ever be a major emphasis in all Church Growth Strategy. Social involvement is no less a part of every valid strategy for church advance. Because of the pressing social needs among urban populations, social involvement assumes particular importance in urban strategy. To preach a loving, caring Christ to a suffering city with no effort to relieve the suffering is hypocrisy. Effective urban patterns will include ministries to the social and physical needs of urban peoples.

Urban patterns must also contain the component of flexibility and creativity. Without the freedom of flexibility, creativity is impossible. In urban church work new ways must be tested. Bold, innovative efforts must be not simply allowed but encouraged. The traditional church-as-usual approach has not proved effective in urban environments. The effective urban church of the future may little resemble the traditional church in structure, method, or plan. While the function of churches will remain solidly biblical, the structure and method may radically change. Such change is possible, probable, and necessary. A flexible and creative approach to urban strategy offers promise of significant advance.

A final component of urban strategy, bold planning, occupies a prominent place in all church growth strategy. In cities church strategy must take notice of demographic patterns, growth directions, and social needs. Urban church workers must be at least as aware of urban needs and trends as are city planners and managers. Urban patterns must be planned in light of understanding of and dedication to cities and their needs. Bold plans, with objectives that can be measured, must be a part of urban strategy. Urban evangelism awaits this bold planning for church growth in the cities.

The Church needs a pattern or patterns for urban ministry. It may well be that the relative lack of growth in urban regions can be attributed partially to the lack of such a pattern or strategy. It is time that Churches and congregations plan specifically for an urban strategy that includes the seven components mentioned. Such a strategy will provide the patterns that will be discussed in the next section.

Patterns for Urban Ministries

Reaching urban areas requires patterns adapted for urban peoples and to urban situations. Establishing these adaptive patterns demands change from traditional methods. The inner-city cathedral church with its lack of neighborhood solidarity, often exhibits a nominal, static, and evangelistically inert nature. Such churches are ineffective in reaching city dwellers. The modern city demands new, boldly different patterns of church ministry. The following suggestions relate to ways churches can develop patterns for urban ministries.

Congruent Congregations

One pattern for urban ministries is congruent congregations. Congruent congregations correspond to the communities in which they exist. The members of congruent churches match the populations of the church neighborhoods. Churches that find significant differences between the socioeconomic status of their members and the communities in which their buildings are located will experience difficulty in attaining adequate, balanced growth.

A certain church found itself in the following situation related to its community. While 68 percent of the community was Black, the church membership was 100 percent White. Over 41 percent of the people in the community worked in jobs requiring manual labor. Only 7 percent of the church members fell in this category. Blue-collar workers, who could be classed as craftsmen or operators, made up 28 percent of the community population but less than 11 percent of the church members. Over 16 percent of the church members were professionals or managers while but 12 percent of the community filled such occupations. The church members could point to 38 percent who had education above high school while the community could find only 16.3 percent in this category. The incongruity is obvious.

This church followed the usual pattern of a church incongruent with its neighborhood. The worship services followed a style that did not appeal to the people living in the area of the church facility. More and more of the members lived in areas away from the church neighborhood and drove back for church activities. The majority of new members came from the remote areas of the church field. The record of growth was a picture of decline. The experience of this church follows a typical pattern for incongruent churches.

Incongruent churches usually center on the needs of the people who have moved away from the neighborhood. Isolation from and animosity toward the different peoples can develop. The people in the community often reject the church as being irrelevant to their situation. The result is a church that seeks merely to survive and loses the opportunity and the urge to minister and grow in the neighborhood of its facility. The incongruent church tends to minister to other communities and neglect its immediate neighborhood.

Achieving congruency is neither automatic nor easy. Conscious effort and positive leadership are required for any movement toward congruency, especially for churches in transitional areas. While difficulties are encountered in attempting to minister simultaneously to both the original members of the church and the new residents of the changing community, it is not impossible. Willis Bennett notes how the Allen Temple Baptist Church of Oakland, California, adapted to reach and minister both to the original members who were living at a distance and the new people who had come into the immediate neighborhood. In a sense Allen Temple Baptist Church moved closer to congruency.[13]

Few churches, and almost no churches in transitional areas, will be congruent with their neighborhoods. The pattern of congruent churches can be attained only as churches consciously identify with the peoples in the areas served. Often the only genuine hope for congruency lies in the provision of new church structures. By whatever means urban strategy must find ways to achieve churches congruent with neighborhood populations.

Multi-People Churches

Churches can sometimes achieve more congruency to the community by using the multi-people approach. In the multi-people approach, one church, bound by brotherly and administrative ties, meets for worship and training in differing groups—each group targeted to satisfy the needs and fit the preferences of a particular segment of the population. Peter Wagner describes this approach in his book, *Our Kind of People.*

The multi-people approach to urban church ministry offers one of the most viable patterns for urban church work. One church, composed of various congregations, each serving language, ethnic, and social groupings, allows stability, finances, shared facilities, brotherhood, and specialized ministry. Interestingly, one critic of Church Growth, after saying that Church Growth Theory has nothing for the city, describes the church the critic himself pastors. The description of his church follows almost precisely the pattern of a multi-people church, one pattern advocated by many Church Growth Writers.[14]

A multi-people church must consciously foster Christian brotherhood and joint action among the various specialized congregations. Most activities will take place in the separate meetings but regular joint celebrations should be provided. There should be a strong sense of unity within the diversity. Any unbalanced financial contribution of one congregation should in no wise involve greater authority or position for that congregation. Contribution should be seen as equal on the "horbitburger pattern." The horbitburger pattern stems from the man who started a restaurant and advertised a "horbitburger." He explained that this burger was made from 50 percent horse and 50 percent rabbit. When asked how he managed exactly 50/50 in the percentage, he answered, "Oh that's easy, I use one horse and one rabbit."

In multi-people churches there is no segregation. Any member from any of the specialized congregations should be free to participate in whatever group he or she desires. The idea is providing for all, not leaving out any.

Multi-people churches provide for the city's diversity and at the same time contribute to brotherhood and mission commitment. Many churches, finding themselves surrounded by different kinds of people whom they are not able to reach with traditional approaches, should consider the multi-people approach. It is a viable option in the urban setting.

Small Group Meetings

Congregations composed of small groups of believers meeting in homes or other settings provide another promising pattern for urban ministry. There is no reason a small group of believers cannot constitute a bonafide church. If the term, "house church" offends, use the expression, "a church that meets in a home." This New Testament pattern (Philem. 2; Rom. 16) promises help in reaching people in apartment complexes, condominiums, and manufactured homes. Church planters have discovered small-group Bible studies and other meetings a productive way to begin churches. The small group approach need not, however, be restricted to the beginning stage of church development. A church may choose to remain a small group, starting other small groups in an effort to evangelize those resistant to larger groups. A house congregation may also be one part of a multi-people church. House churches should be accorded the dignity of full acceptance by the denomination, be considered full and complete churches, and be allowed to express their faith through the observation of baptism, the Lord's Supper, and any other church function.

Calvin (Cal) Guy contends that the house church approach holds great potential for reaching the cities. Since, he says, the "big building" approach has not reached the urban poor, this different pattern should be encouraged. Of the house church, Guy says:

> The poverty of the urban masses, their inability to erect and support large structures, and the psychology of the urban poor that prevents them from identification with large numbers of people, point to the small group and the house church as the most feasible approach. In the small, caring communities

> where Christians listen to the Word, share the sacraments, uphold one another in prayer, and witness verbally and visibly to their neighbors, it may be that the faith will flow as in the first century to the great urban populations.[15]

Small-group methods in the form of Bible studies, discussion groups, action groups, and other expressions hold promise for urban church growth. No theological aversion should blind church leaders to the advisibility and practicality of the small-group approach. Small group methods are a valid urban pattern.

Total Body Ministry

Effective urban patterns, like all other effective church ministry, must employ the entire body of the church. Every member should be recruited, motivated, and trained for the ministry in the urban environment. Sidney H. Rooy correctly assesses the situation, saying:

> To fulfill its goal of reconciliation, urban theological education should prepare Christians to carry out a shared ministry that incorporates each member according to his gifts into the preaching, conversion, and healing service, both within the local spiritual brotherhood and in the broader community of which it is a part.[16]

The total body ministry follows the plan of Ephesians 4:11-13. Should a church be able to hire a staff that could perform all the witness, all the service, all the comfort, all the teaching, all the influence needed in the community, this would still not be the biblical way. To be congruent with biblical standards, the entire body of the church must function in ministry. The idea that the membership supports the church staff that does the ministry is perhaps the greatest heresy in present-day church life.

Urban churches must train members to participate actively in all phases of church ministry. Every spiritual gift should be discovered and used in order that every need be met. Total body ministry constitutes one of the more viable patterns for urban church ministry.

Satellite Churches

The original area and a new ministry area can be reached simultaneously by using the satellite church pattern. This pattern allows one congregation and one church staff. The church remains to serve both the original members and the new residents in the church neighborhood. It also provides for people in a new area of ministry. The satellite pattern has been used successfully and while it does involve some problems holds promise for urban ministries.

Relationship Patterns

Urban ministry can effectively use the relationship pattern of witness as suggested in chapter two. Following relational lines may have special relevance in the city where people tend to settle near family and friends. Charles Chaney and Don Lewis suggest a "Productive Prospect Search Form" which helps Christians recognize their "relationships" and thereby visualize their most promising prospects.[17]

Urban churches must often serve a varied geographical and social environment. Relationship lines provide a means of both evangelizing and shepherding people in the anonymity of the city. The relationship pattern can be incorporated into every phase of the church activity. Small groups can best be organized along relational lines. Here then is another possibility for effective urban ministry.

Multi-faceted Ministry

Urban patterns call for a variety of approaches to meet a variety of needs. Every urban problem, from poverty to crime, holds a possibility for urban church ministry. Urban ministry should engage in a multi-faceted approach in order to address the spiritual, physical, and psychological needs of city dwellers. Bennett cites the variety of ministries as the key to the growth of the Allen Temple Baptist Church. Bennett declares:

> Some churches in transitional communities function like small islands, isolated from the larger community. This does not appear to be true of Allen Temple. They continue to be able to appeal to people who live nearby, while still able to reach to the larger community. The appeal comes through the wide variety of ministries provided, and to the worship services which are theologically and culturally relevant to the growing congregation.[18]

Churches in the city must seize the opportunities of the urban environment and devise a variety of ministries to meet these needs.

Conclusion

Cities provide possibilities for significant church growth. Every denomination and Mission must strive to develop patterns for reaching and serving the cities. Every effort must be expended to create congruent congregations to reach city areas. The city is no more evil than any other place. Because it encompasses great numbers of people in smaller areas, its problems are intensified. This fact only means that ministry to cities must be expanded—both in magnitude and effectiveness.

Questions and Activities

1. Discuss, pro and con, the following statement, "In the period between now and AD 2000, missions should be dedicated totally to urban areas."
2. List the components of a sound urban strategy.
3. Visit a church that is operating on the multi-people pattern; on the satellite church pattern. What are your impressions?
4. Visit an area of a city where the underprivileged live. Do the churches seem to be helping the people?
5. Can the church reach the inner-city?

Further Reading

Roger S. Greenway, ed. *Discipling the Cities* (Baker)
G. Willis Bennett, *Effective Urban Church Ministry* (Broadman)
Larry Rose and C. Kirk Hadaway, *The Urban Challenge* (Broadman)
Stanley D. Brunn and Jack F. Williams, *Cities of the World* (Harper and Row)
Ronald D. Pasquariella, Donald W. Shriver, Jr., and Alan Geyer, *Redeeming the City* (The Pilgrim Press)
Benjamin Tonna, *Gospel for the Cities* (Orbis)

Notes

1. Donald A. McGavran, *Understanding Church Growth,* p. 332.
2. Roger Greenway, "Mission to an Urban World," *Urban Mission* 1, 1 (September 1983):1.
3. Ralph H. Elliott, "Dangers of the Church Growth Movement," *The Christian Century,* August 12-19, 1981, p. 801.
4. Larry Rose and C. Kirk Hadaway, "Toward An Urban Awareness," in *The Urban Challenge,* ed. Larry L. Rose and C. Kirk Hadaway (Nashville: Broadman Press, 1982), p. 16.
5. Stanley D. Brunn and Jack F. Williams, *Cities of the World: World Regional Urban Development* (New York: Harper and Row, Publishers, 1983), p. 10.

6. Ibid., p. 12.

7. Rose and Hadaway, p. 17 (quoting from *Patterns of Urban and Rural Population Growth* (New York: United Nations, 1980).

8. Johannes F. Linn, *Cities in the Developing World* (Washington, D.C.: Oxford University Press, 1983), p. xiv.

9. Ibid., pp. 150-51.

10. Paul Geisel, "Understanding American Cities," in *The Urban Challenge,* ed. Larry Rose and C. Kirk Hadaway, p. 31.

11. Larry L. Rose and C. Kirk Hadaway, "Toward an Urban Awareness," pp. 18-19.

12. G. Willis Bennett, *Effective Urban Church Ministry* (Nashville: Broadman Press, 1983), p. 167.

13. Ibid., p. 117.

14. Ralph H. Elliott, *Church Growth that Counts,* pp. 11-12.

15. Calvin Guy, "Pilgrimage Toward the House Church," in *Discipling the City,* ed. Roger S. Greenway (Grand Rapids: Baker Book House, 1979), p. 127.

16. Sidney H. Rooy, "Theological Education for Urban Mission," in *Discipling the City,* ed. Roger S. Greenway, p. 185.

17. Charles Chaney and Don Lewis, *Design for Church Growth* (Nashville: Broadman Press, 1977), p. 216.

18. Bennett, p. 117.

9
Leading Through Servanthood

The world has invaded the church. One area of this invasion unfortunately has gone practically unnoticed. This unrecognized invasion lies in the area of churches' and church people's attitudes toward success and leadership style. Some Christians and Churches have adopted a basically worldly approach to success and leadership. Worse still, they often teach this worldly view of success and leadership as *the biblical way.*

Church growth is uniquely and intimately tied to leadership—both pastoral and lay. Churches with growth-oriented leadership grow whole churches with leadership not committed to growth stagnate or decline. Balanced church growth and aggressive, dedicated growth-oriented leadership are inextricably tied together. Churches and church leaders who make the most lasting contributions to God's kingdom and church growth are those, however, who eschew the world's standards and patterns and lead through the biblical model of servanthood. Effective, lasting, and genuine church growth depends basically on both Christians and churches accepting and practicing the servant pattern of ministry.

The servant pattern consists of living, leading, and acting on behalf of others. In the biblical sense, servants turn away from demanding their needs be met and seek ways of meeting the needs of others. The servant pattern refuses to manipulate, coerce, or force. The central purpose of servant leadership remains the benefit of the served.

The Biblical Model

The nature of the servant pattern is best understood by an investigation of the biblical model. The creation of God's special people, Israel, pictures the concept of servanthood. Abraham and his people were called, not in order to become a great nation, but rather to become a blessing to the nations (Gen. 12:1-3). The promise of blessing and greatness were steps to enable Israel to become the "Servant."

The book of Jonah relates directly to Israel's loss of the servant pattern. Israel as a nation had forgotten its mission to be the channel of God's blessings. She had become self-centered, concerned only with what God would do for her. Jonah's anger at God's forgiving Nineveh and the turning of his wrath is symbolic of the loss of Israel's servant attitude.

Churches, Missions, denominations, and church leaders today can fall into the sin of Israel during Jonah's time. The eclipse of the servant pattern leads Christians and Christian institutions to lose compassion and ministry. Loss of the servant attitude leads to selfish seeking of personal or church advance. Jonah pictures the people of God without the servant attitude.

The nature of the "Servant" in Isaiah pictures the model of the servant pattern of ministry. The Servant lived not for the Servant's benefit but the Servant met the needs of others by establishing justice (Isa. 42: 1-4). The Servant people, Israel, existed for the purpose of serving others by making God known to them:

> And now says the Lord, who formed Me from the womb to be His Servant, / to bring Jacob back to Him, in order that Israel might be gathered to Him / (For I am honored in the sight of the Lord, / And My God is My strength), / He says, "It is too small a thing that You should be My Servant / To raise up the tribes of Jacob, and to restore the preserved ones of Israel; / I will also make You a light of the nations / So that My salvation may reach to the end of the earth" (Isa. 49:5-6, NASB).

Nowhere is the servant motif more clearly stated than in Isaiah 53:

> Surely our griefs He Himself bore, / And our sorrows He carried; / Yet we ourselves esteemed Him stricken, / Smitten of God, and afflicted. / But He was pierced through for our transgressions, / He was crushed for our iniquities; / The chastening for our well-being fell upon Him, / And by His scourging we are healed. / All of us like sheep have gone astray, / Each of us has turned to his own way; / But the Lord has caused the iniquity of us all / To fall on Him (Isa. 53:4-6, NASB).

The incarnation of Christ remains the overriding model of the servant pattern. Jesus himself pointed to the "Servant" as the model of his mission (Luke 4:1-4). The wonder of the self-emptying of Christ for the purpose of serving is pictured in the beautiful hymn in Philippians 2:5-11. The Lord declared his way to be the way of servanthood: "For even the Son of Man did not come to be served, but to serve and to give His life a ransom for many" (Mark 10:45, NASB).

The world's way is to "lord over" and "be the authority over." The servant way is to die to self and to serve others. Jesus exemplified the servant pattern in the upper room as he washed the disciples' feet (John 13:1-15).

The servant pattern is based on self-denial and commitment to others (Luke 9:23-27). Self-denial and cross-bearing refer to more than physical hardship or suffering. The major impact of dying to self as it relates to servanthood is well stated by L. H. Marshall who says that Jesus

> makes self-denial the first condition of discipleship, "If any man wishes to come after me, let him deny himself" (Matt. 16:24). Here the reference is not to petty acts of what is commonly called "self-denial," but to something far more drastic. The axe is to be laid at the very root of the tree of evil, namely, excessive love of self; life is no longer to revolve round the self as its centre, but round the love of God and the love of man; self is to be torn from life's throne, and God and neighbor are to be put in its place; love is no longer to be a mere centripetal force—directed wholy inwards, to the self; it is also to be a centrifugal force—directed outwards to God and man; there is to be a radical change in interest and care, which, instead of being concentrated on the self, are to be lavished on God and man. To "deny oneself," therefore, is to recognize, acknowledge and accept the claims of God and of one's fellowmen, to subordinate self-interest to the love of God and man. This idea of "self-denial" was something new in Ethics, and self-sacrifice for the sake of others, as a means to social good, is the central ideal of Christian morality.[1]

Calvary epitomizes servanthood as the sinless Son of God laid down his life for sinful mankind. We must never view the cross as defeat which was reversed by the victory of resurrection. The cross, gladly and willingly borne, was in itself victory. Those who wish to follow the Lord's example must follow him to the cross—and in this death will find true life (Luke 9:23-26).

Important to this discussion is the beautiful teaching of Jesus that fruitfulness in God's kingdom depends on the degree of "dying to self" on the disciple's part:

> Now there were certain Greeks among those who were going up to worship at the feast; these therefore came to Philip, who was from Bethsaida of Galilee, and began to ask him, saying, "Sir, we wish to see Jesus." Philip came and told Andrew; Andrew and Philip came, and they told Jesus. And Jesus answered them, saying, "The hour has come for the Son of Man to be glorified. Truly, truly, I say to you, unless a grain of wheat falls into the earth and dies, it remains by itself alone; but if it dies, it bears much fruit. He who loves his life

> loses it; and he who hates his life in this world shall keep it to life eternal. If anyone serves Me, let him follow Me; and where I am, there shall My servant also be; if any one serves Me, the Father will honor him. Now My soul has become troubled; and what shall I say, "Father, save me from this hour"? But for this purpose I came to this hour. "Father, glorify Thy name." There came therefore a voice out of heaven: "I have both glorified it, and will glorify it again" (John 12:20-28, NASB).

Clearly, the servant pattern leads to fruitfulness; the absence of the servant pattern produces the tragedy of fruitlessness. To serve God and man and bring forth fruit requires the adoption of the servant pattern. To the degree we die to self, we produce fruit in God's kingdom and authentic church growth.

Leadership, according to the biblical model, uses the servant pattern. Balanced church growth can be realized only through servant leadership. It is, therefore, imperative that those seeking God's kind of church growth adopt the servant pattern of leadership.

The Expression of Servant Pattern Leadership

Servanthood on the biblical model must be expressed or lived out for balanced church growth to occur. This expression of the servant pattern takes place in the real world where men and women are won and shepherded in vital, growing churches. We will turn our attention on how the servant pattern can be expressed in daily efforts toward church growth.

This section investigates how the servant pattern can and should be expressed in church leadership. The thesis is that authoritative, manipulative, driving, controlling, leader-dominated patterns are neither biblical nor productive of genuine church growth. Headship involves service not dominance or control. The servant pattern expresses itself in special types of leadership.

Relationship Rather Than Position

The servant pattern conceives of leadership as based on relationship rather than position. Biblical headship of pastor or church leader turns away from authoritarian patterns that coerce, to relational patterns that lead for the benefit of the one guided. The concept of a position that demands obedience and submission is foreign to the biblical concept of headship.

Speaking of the passage in Ephesians 5:21-33, Richards and Hoeldtke take issue with views of headship that suggest authoritarian or dictatorial patterns. They write:

> If we are ever tempted to extend this analogy to suggest authoritarian roles for church leaders, we will be driven by the biblical data to the position that leadership involves our giving ourselves up for those we serve (v. 25) and committing ourselves as holy and blameless expressions of Jesus to the fulfillment of the Christian community and the Christian individual. We surely find no basis here for claiming a position of authority over the church or for claiming a right to make decisions and command obedience. If there is any basis for human leaders to claim such a control or command a position in the church, that basis must be found somewhere other than in the New Testament presentation of headship.[2]

Some have understood C. Peter Wagner to be advocating authoritarianism on the part of a pastor.[3] I personally think that Wagner has overused the word authority and would have done well to use concepts of servant. Fairness to all demands, however, that it be noted that Wagner speaks of authority earned through love and living relationship with the people.[4] Wagner is not advocating a dictator nor an authoritarian seeking his own ways and needs. He is stressing the importance of adequate pastoral leadership.

Church growth depends on adequate leadership. Pastor and church leaders must be "possibility thinkers." Motivation towards goals is indispensable. Church leaders must accept and live out responsibility. This leadership should be relational—based on living contact and vital concern for those led. It should never be simply positional—demanding regard, obedience, following due to the position of the pastor or other church leaders.

Service Rather Than Control

The servant pattern seeks to serve rather than demand service. The goal of servant leadership is support and lift rather than control. The concern of the servant is for others. The servant develops a willingness to seek the welfare of others and the practice of giving rather than demanding. Self-giving, not control, is basic to servanthood.

Genuine servanthood avoids the error of paternalism. Missionaries can easily fall into control patterns based on their experience, responsibilities for funds, and training. Genuine concern for the work can lead to false patterns of leadership resulting in control. Servant leadership exchanges control methods for service methods. Roy Edgemon says:

> Jesus made it clear that the practical consequence of love is always service. He was trying to help them understand that he was there to serve and he loved them enough to do what they refused to do.[5]

The motivation for service in the servant pattern is always love. Love turns away from methods that manipulate or use others and seeks only to meet the needs of the object of love. Love eschews any temptation to use others to further one's own interests. Rather the motive of the servant's life becomes service that grows out of love.

Equipping Rather Than Performing

Servant leadership recognizes that equipping rather than performing leads to more lasting and balanced church growth. Paul's message concerning church leaders indicates that church leaders (apostles, prophets, evangelists, pastors, teachers) are given for the purpose of equipping God's people (the saints) for the work of ministry (service) to the end of building up the body of Christ (Eph. 4:11-13). Thus, the Bible establishes the equipping ministry pattern.

Church Growth writers have consistently emphasized the place of the laity.[6] Those who feel that Wagner placed too great emphasis on pastoral leadership, need to read his chapter which emphasizes the place of the laity.[7] Balanced church growth results when ministry is the shared responsibility of the entire body, the church. Even if a church could secure enough staff to fulfill all witnessing and ministry requirements, this would not be the biblical pattern. Authentic church growth demands the total incorporation of the entire church in the constant outworking of the ministry.

The realization of the key place laypeople hold in church growth led Donald A. McGavran to develop the concept of five classes of leaders.[8] Class five leaders, he says, are denominational leaders. These leaders are important to church growth but not too many are necessary. Class four leaders are fully trained, fully paid, full-time church staff workers. As seen earlier, these leaders fill a vital and imperative role in church growth. The pastor and staff can either motivate the church and enhance its ministry or stand in the way of genuine growth.

Class three leaders are part-time church workers. The term *bivocational* often describes these leaders. Class three leaders hold vast importance for church growth and should be honored and used in greatly increasing numbers. The evangelization of the world depends on the use of thousands of bivocational workers. Tendencies to view bivocational workers less important and to some degree exclude them from fellowship with full-time workers must be discarded. Far from being a second-best, second-rate minister, the bivocational worker is one of the more promising possibilities for world mission.

The last two groups of workers, class one and two, are both unpaid, voluntary workers. They differ, however, in the direction of their ministries. Class one workers relate primarily to the church and its own needs. These workers are the members of building and grounds committee, finance committee, ushers, choir, teachers and etc. They are important and necessary to the church and its work. Their number should increase as should their dedication and training.

Class two workers have their ministry primarily among the unsaved outside the church. Their efforts go to reach the lost in the world and bring them into the church. Conversion growth is the primary goal of class two workers.

The problem in most churches is that the lion's share of workers and time goes into class one type work with little time and few workers committed to class two efforts. Studies of churches indicate that the usual pattern is that 96 to 98 percent of the church's workers and work hours are dedicated to class one work. Little wonder conversion growth lags!

The local church that desires balanced, authentic growth must pray that class two workers are raised up. These workers must be trained and motivated for continuous witness. Doubling the class two workers and work will lead to increased church growth.

As local churches must emphasize class two workers, denominations must emphasize class three workers. Most denominations provide extensive and expensive programs for training class four and class five type workers. Little emphasis and less money is committed to training class three, bivocational ministers. At least one third of the denominational resources for leadership training should be committed to the training of bivocational workers, especially in developing countries. Existing training schools (seminaries, Bible colleges, etc.) should include vocational training to enable graduates to become bivocational. Bivocational, class three ministers and ministries should be encouraged by any denomination that aspires to authentic church growth.

The methods related to theological education by extension are available today to help train all workers. These methods of training are especially effective for bivocational workers. Authentic church growth makes full use of class three workers and provides for their training and service.

Servant leadership thus seeks to develop, rather than drive, lay Christians. Church members are helped to discover, develop, and employ their spiritual gifts. The servant pattern consists of serving alongside rather than performing service for others.

The Tragedy of Absence of the Servant Pattern

Servanthood is sometimes tragically missing in the lives of church leaders. Ministry, on the part of the church staff and the part of volunteer workers, can be performed for selfish, tainted reasons. Desire for personal recognition, material gain, status, prestige, or position drive some to Christian leadership methods that depart from the servant pattern. I think such leaders were in Paul's mind when he warned Timothy of certain men, saying:

> If anyone advocates a different doctrine, and does not agree with sound words, those of our Lord Jesus Christ, and with the doctrine conforming to godliness, he is conceited and understands nothing; but he has a morbid interest in controversial questions and disputes about words, out of which arise envy, strife, abusive language, evil suspicions, and constant friction between men of depraved mind and deprived of the truth, who suppose that godliness is a means of gain. But godliness actually is a means of great gain, when accompanied by contentment (1 Tim. 6:3-6, NASB).

The tragedy of the absence of the servant pattern is several fold. The leader misses the blessing and reward of genuine service. The rewards of service are negligible or missing altogether. The Christian movement loses respect in the eyes of unbelivers. God's people are driven rather than led. The pattern of Jesus is replaced by the way of the world and God's work is blocked by mankind's misguided ambition.

Anytime the concept of success is tied totally to ideas of bigness, power, recognition, material gain, the servant pattern is endangered. Churches as well as pastors can fall victim to the sin of substituting ambition, desire for first place, recognition, outward success, financial stability for the servant pattern. Drive to quick success can lead to short-cut methods and inauthentic results. The servant pattern refuses to compromise genuine growth.

Charles Swindoll, commenting on Jesus' statement, "whoever wishes to become great among you shall be your servant" (Matt. 20:26, NASB), declares that these words seem to be forgotten:

> Even in many churches with their smooth pastors, high powered executives, and superstar singers. Unfortunately, there doesn't seem to be much of the servant mentality in such settings. Even in our church life we tend to get so caught up in a success and size race that we lose sight of our primary calling as followers of Christ. The "celebrity syndome" so present in our Christian thought and activities just doesn't square with the attitudes and messages of Jesus. We have skidded into a pattern whereby the celebrities and top dogs in our church life call the shots, and it is difficult to be a servant when you're used to telling others what to do.[9]

The self-pattern, the antithesis of servant pattern, can often creep almost unnoticed into church life or into the thinking of church leaders. Once in the church (or the church leader) the self-attitude often remains undetected creating inauthentic ministry. There are ways, however, to detect the self-spirit. The self-pattern might be suspected when in the life of the church or leader:

- Equipment becomes more important than ministry. If buildings, vans, degrees, TV programs become ends rather than means one might suspect self-pattern.
- Requests for funds and support overshadow searches for ways to serve.
- Local interests outweigh kingdom needs. If local budget or capital needs cancels mission giving or the local church spends on self rather than missionary outreach.
- The leader insists on agreement and is outraged at opposition to his plans.
- When leaders and churches are quick to take offense at any criticism or encroachment on their "territory."
- When leaders and churches refrain from or refuse to take a stand on unpopular issues.
- When undue effort is expended to draw attention to self or to local church.
- When growth is demanded and attained regardless of the methods or the reality of the growth.
- When reports of "success" are exaggerated or broadcast and records of reversal suppressed or denied.

The absence of servant pattern leadership and church life crushes balanced church growth. It is, therefore, imperative that leaders and churches follow the example of the Master and adopt the servant pattern.

Adopting the Servant Pattern

Balanced church growth becomes a reality when churches and leaders adopt the servant pattern. How can one be sure he or she is leading through servanthood? How can one adopt this servant pattern?

A foremost method of becoming a servant lies in the exercise of faith. The conviction that God, through his Spirit, will bring to pass through us both the needs of others and our own needs stimulates toward the servant pattern. When faith is weak, human action and efforts seek to be certain that credit is given, position respected, and rewards bestowed. Only those of deep faith adopt the servant pattern, believing that "whoever wishes to save his life shall lose it; but whoever loses his life for My sake shall find it" (Matt. 16:25, NASB).

Developing proper attitudes toward material matters, money, possessions, reputations, and power can aid the adoption of the servant attitude. Jesus placed the material in proper perspective and this perspective opens the way to servanthood. Refusing to allow material considerations to determine style of ministry likewise protects against departing from the servant pattern.

Placing people first helps churches and leaders adopt the servant pattern. All persons are created in the image of God. All are important. When people are foremost, equipment, personal profit or fame, or church position become less vital. Proper emphasis on people enhances servanthood and, consequently, balanced church growth.

Accepting the nature of genuine growth stimulates following the servant pattern. Only growth that leads to responsible, growing, reproducing Christians in responsible, growing, reproducing churches is genuine church growth. The self-pattern can produce a false form of growth; only the servant pattern will lead to genuine balanced growth.

Following the example of Jesus leads to the servant attitude. When he was cursed, he answered nothing but gave his life a ransom for many. Servanthood consists of following his example.

Finally, commitment to him and his pattern eventuates in the servant pattern. Dying to self cannot be accomplished by the effort of any person. Dying to self comes only through the commitment that asks and allows the Holy Spirit to cleanse from sin, save from self, and separate for service. If a person lives to the flesh (by the self-principle), that person dies, loses all. If, by the Spirit, a person puts to death the deeds of the body (self), that person lives (Rom. 8:13). This commitment remains the ultimate way to attain servanthood.

Conclusion

The servant pattern promotes authentic church growth. All who desire that churches continue to grow bigger, better, and broader, as people are won to Christ and grow in him, will allow this pattern to be created in them by the Spirit. Leading through servanthood constitutes the supreme strategy for authentic church growth.

Questions and Activities

1. Read Isaiah 40—55. List the qualities of "the Servant." Suggest ways leaders today can adopt this pattern.
2. Study your church's leadership. How many persons and person-hours are devoted to Class I and Class II ministry?
3. Describe the difference in authoritative "headship" and "Servant" headship.
4. What is the meaning of "dying to self"? How does one "die to self"?
5. Describe the ideal church leader—both a pastor and non-staff leader.

Further reading

Ralph Neighbour, *Future Church* (Broadman)
Charles R. Swindoll, *Improving Your Serve* (Word)
L. H. Marshall, *The Challenge of New Testament Ethics* (St. Martin's Press)
T. B. Maston, *Why Live the Christian Life?* (Thomas Nelson)
C. Peter Wagner, *Leading Your Church to Grow* (Regal)

Notes

1. L. H. Marshall, *The Challenge of New Testament Ethics* (London: St. Martin's Press, 1956), p. 35.

2. Lawrence O. Richards and Clyde Hoeldtke, *A Theology of Church Leadership* (Grand Rapids: Zondervan, 1980), p. 22.

3. C. Peter Wagner, *Your Church Can Grow,* pp. 57-68.

4. Ibid., p. 59.

5. Ralph Neighbour, *Future Church* (Nashville: Broadman Press, 1980), p. 32.

6. Donald A. McGavran and Winfield C. Arn, *Ten Steps for Church Growth,* pp. 108-109.

7. Wagner, *Your Church Can Grow,* pp. 69-83.

8. McGavran and Arn, *Ten Steps for Church Growth,* pp. 108-109.

9. Charles R. Swindoll, *Improving Your Serve* (Waco: Word Books, 1981), pp. 21-27.

Conclusion

Balanced church growth is not only the imperative goal of Christian ministry, it is the only possible goal. Adequate power for reaching the goal is available. The time is now. God's people must reach toward the fullest meaning of balanced church growth.

Balanced, authentic church growth can never be attained by mechanically instituting business or corporation techniques into the life of churches. No methodology automatically produces genuine church growth in either numbers or quality. To even suggest that church growth would consider the mechanical use of techniques and expect growth is to overlook the spiritual and biblical foundation on which church growth thinking is built.

Authentic church growth points to disciple-making, church planting, and continuous harvest. The goal, responsible, reproducing Christians in responsible, reproducing churches, can only be reached as Christians and churches allow the Holy Spirit to lead them to more effective ways (strategies) of winning people to Christ and incorporating them into vital congregations. Authentic church growth sees the Holy Spirit active in the entire process. He motivates to growth, leads to methods for growth, provides the power to grow, grants the increase of growth, and continues the process of growth.

Authentic church growth uses only methods that can be tested and proved as congruent with biblical teachings. Every strategy must be biblical both in its application and result. Church growth may use techniques adopted from the business world, from behavioral sciences, and from other disciplines but will test these strategies and their results by the biblical standard.

Authentic church growth can only be attained through the servant pattern. Self-seeking, authoritarian, unloving approaches produce invalid growth. The servant pattern allows for the God-kind of growth. Authentic church growth seeks the winning and discipling of people to and in him, the planting and developing of churches, and the continuing outreach to all the people of the world.